PREPARE FOR DISASTER

THE ONE BOOK YOU NEED TO PLAN FOR EMERGENCIES

By **JAMES D. LEE, P.E.**
STEVE HEALY, B.S., M.S.
MARC LEE, M.S., M.E.

About The Authors:
50 years of combined experience.
U.S. Military and Homeland Security experts who consult on chemical, biological, radiological and nuclear risk management—the team of experts to trust.

PREPARE
FOR
DISASTER
THE ONE BOOK YOU NEED
TO PLAN FOR EMERGENCIES

Correspondence concerning this book may be directed to the publisher at the address above.

ISBN: 0794836607

Printed in China

To view other products from Whitman Publishing, please visit www.Whitman.com.

All illustrations by Tim Hynes.

All photographs provided by Shutterstock.com.

Contents

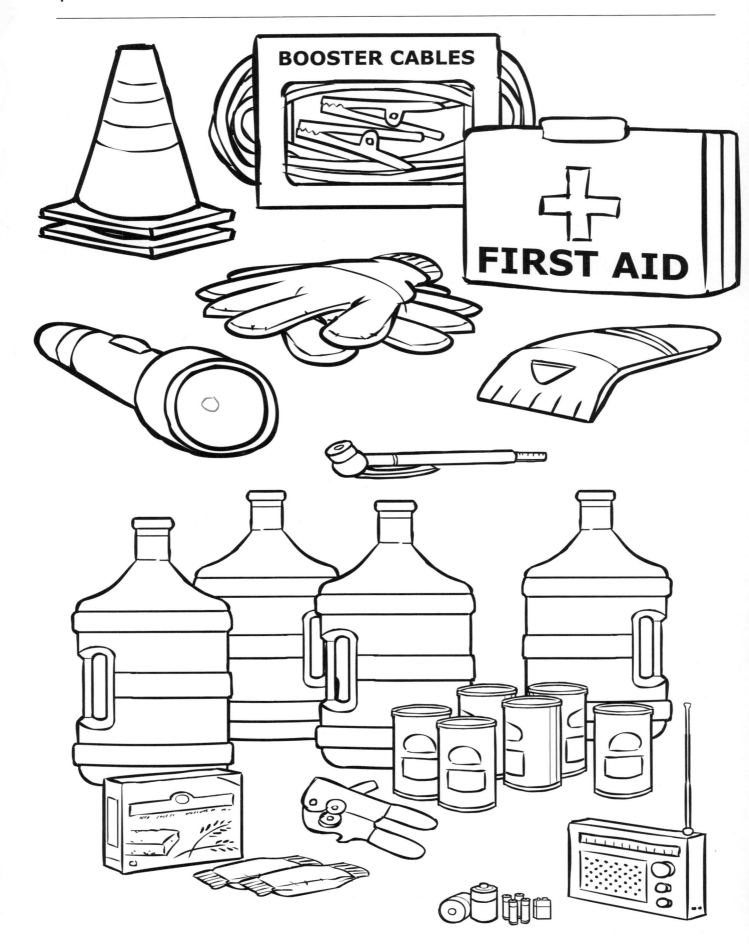

BOOSTER CABLES

FIRST AID

Prepare For Disaster

This book will serve as a guide to help you decide what to do if an emergency event is forecast to strike or actually strikes when you are at home or at work. You will learn simple, achievable and inexpensive ways to better prepare you and your family to respond to a variety of emergency events.

While no one can tell us the time and place of each emergency event, everyone can plan their response "just in case." Preparation is the key, from developing your family emergency plan, to the supplies you have stored to shelter-in-place and those supplies packed for evacuating to a safer place.

You may find that you have already taken some of our recommended steps, and that's great! But this book will help you identify additional steps so you can complete a comprehensive response plan for you and your family. For some of you, this may be a new issue of vital importance and you need ideas on how to get started. This book will help you be prepared for any emergency event.

Each chapter will provide you with specific steps to help you prepare for and respond to an emergency.

Let's move on to Chapter 1 and start our preparations.

Chapter 1: Preparing for an Emergency

SCAN FOR CHAPTER OVERVIEW VIDEO

"There are risks and costs to a program of action. But they are far less than the long-range risks and costs of comfortable inaction."

— *President John F. Kennedy*

We will all face different kinds of emergencies during our lives. The emergencies can come in many shapes and sizes — from a severe thunderstorm with localized flooding to a hurricane impacting millions of people across tens of thousands of square miles.

We believe that there will be some form of government assistance to help us through emergencies. Federal, state and local authorities have established emergency plans to assist you in your area. However, these plans represent the intent to help, not a guarantee of action. We do not know how much help we will actually get, when it will come and if it will meet our needs.

We are not in control of these emergencies or in the government's reaction, but we are in control of our preparations and response. Now is time to prepare.

Before an emergency occurs, make a plan and build your emergency kits. When a potential emergency has been identified or an emergency suddenly develops, stay informed, take action and communicate those actions.

MAKE A PLAN

Start with your plan. Are you part of a family living together or are you single? Family members who are not present can't help with the family's immediate actions, but they are part of the family's communications plan and may provide options if the family needs to temporarily relocate.

If you are single, we recommend using the buddy system — consider your friends as the family you choose. This becomes especially important when you are living away from your family and do not have their ready support.

Build your individual plan and talk with your friends about it. Who do you want watching your back during an emergency? Who has a critical skill set that your group could benefit from? Who believes in preparing ahead of time? Their response and their actions (do they actually build their own emergency kit, for example) will guide your decision to depend on them in an emergency.

Small groups will survive an emergency better than an individual. A group, whether related by blood or chosen, will help each other when someone is hurt or unable to get to safety on their own.

You can even form a group of family and friends, but the key is to plan ahead!

GROUP DECISIONS

First, you need to identify your group — family related by blood, group related by friendship, or a mix of family and friends.

A group needs leaders, and everyone must agree to act as a team, otherwise the group is just a cluster of individuals who are pretending. This will not work when an emergency occurs. If a person, even one with skills you value, cannot act for the good of the group, it is better to let them go their own way and not depend on them. This is not about having one person rule a group, but rather having the group agree that after brief discussion, they either vote to follow majority rule or choose one of their number to decide for the group. Agree how group decisions will be made and put it in your plan.

The plan should also identify two people who will get in touch with the local and long-distance contacts with the decision to shelter-in-place or evacuate.

COMMUNICATIONS
CELL PHONES

Communication is critical, so let's start with our cell phones.

Go into your contact list and identify those contacts that you would call in an emergency by putting "ICE" (In Case of Emergency) in front of their names. If children have cell phones, repeat this step so everyone has identified emergency contacts.

Next, identify the primary local contact everyone would call if there is an emergency. This person can be identified as "ICE1" on everyone's cell phone contact list. Then identify the long-distance contact everyone would notify so that one person — preferably not in the area affected by the emergency — would be able to receive everyone's calls and relay instructions as needed. This person can be identified as "ICE9" in everyone's cell phones. Additional local and long-distance contacts can be identified in the same way ("ICE2" and "ICE8," for example).

It is important to remember that text messaging may still work when network disruptions stop phone calls from getting through. Therefore, teach everyone how to create, send and receive text messages.

Local & Long-Distance Contacts

Make sure that any local and long-distance contacts understand their role — what they need to do in case of a potential emergency.

Local contacts may be best used for immediate communication and initial coordination, for example, who is picking up which child at what school or who is meeting where, with what vehicle and supplies.

Long-distance contacts may be best used for long-term coordination and updates on the status of the emergency. If you choose to or must evacuate, they can help identify the status of different evacuation routes so that you are better able to avoid massive traffic jams and road closures due to the emergency.

Schools & Daycare

For those of you with children in daycare or school, ask the childcare provider/school for a copy of their emergency plan. This information will be critical if you have little to no warning of an emergency. How will the daycare or school communicate when they are closing, and have they tested their ability to reach you? Ensure they have up-to-date contact information for your family so you can be reached.

ALERTS

Subscribe to your community's alert services. Many communities now offer the ability to sign up for email and/or text message alerts if there is an emergency. This can help you stay informed while you are traveling locally, and add to what you are hearing from television and radio broadcasts if you are at home or at work.

The following website has state and local information that can also help you stay informed: http://www.ready.gov/community-state-info.

SOCIAL MEDIA

Social media is focused on interactive communication — sharing information using the Internet.

There are many different social media applications, including Facebook and Twitter. These applications allow us to change how we communicate. They take us beyond simply receiving information from TV or radio, or calling one person at a time. When you post information on Facebook, you reach many people at once. When you use Twitter, you provide real-time information to a group of people.

Consider your family or group when deciding if social media would improve your ability to communicate with each other.

WHERE TO MEET

If you are part of a group or family, you will need to agree on where to meet in case of an emergency. While a family will likely gather where they live, a group will have to agree on where to meet.

The group could identify two locations to meet based on the actions they will take: one place may be best suited to shelter-in-place while the second, with better access to highways, is the designated place to meet and evacuate from. Put your decisions in your plan.

SHELTER-IN-PLACE OR EVACUATE?

Do you stay or do you leave? This is an important decision your group must make in response to an emergency.

Some emergencies, like an oncoming hurricane, can give plenty of warning time before they happen. Other emergencies, like a terrorist attack or an industrial accident, can occur without warning, thus leaving no time to evacuate, so you must shelter-in-place for immediate protection.

Here are some important points to guide your decision to stay or go.

- The need to shelter-in-place: Is there a danger to leaving the local area, your home or workplace? Would you be in more danger if you evacuated than if you stayed? Is there a medical reason that prevents you from leaving?
- The need to evacuate: Do you have enough advance warning to evacuate? Is there an immediate danger (fire or flooding) to staying? Would you be in more danger if you stayed than if you evacuated?

Three "Yes" answers in either category would be a strong signal to act accordingly.

You must add in your own circumstances to the questions above and decide: Do we stay or do we leave? If you choose to evacuate, it is better to leave before the authorities order an evacuation. In a crowd evacuation (one encouraged by the authorities), you may only be able to leave at the speed of the crowd. You will be more limited because you will be traveling with many people who have not prepared for the emergency. This will reduce the effectiveness of your own preparations and make it more difficult to reach your evacuation destination.

BUILD YOUR EMERGENCY KITS

Do you keep a first-aid kit and a blanket in your vehicle for emergencies? What about a few water bottles and snack food? When you put these together, you are on your way to building your emergency travel kit. Do you keep a cell-phone charger in the vehicle? Your ability to communicate is critical, so adding a charger is another key item in your travel kit.

You will need to prepare two emergency kits. One, your travel kit, will stay in the vehicle in case you are caught on the road when the emergency strikes. The second kit is larger, with more supplies to help you shelter-in-place.

EMERGENCY TRAVEL KIT

This kit stays in your vehicle. It is like the spare tire you keep in your trunk: you do not want to use it, but you keep it there just in case of an emergency. While each vehicle in a family or group should have some emergency supplies in it, you will need to decide whether or not to keep an emergency travel kit in multiple cars. This kit should include more than some food, water and a flashlight. It should meet your needs and the needs of your family or group.

Does anyone in your group need prescription drugs (or an epi-pen for an allergy to bee stings, for example)? Keep an up-to-date list of prescriptions. See Appendix 1 for a suggested list of medicines for your emergency kit. Look at anything in your medicine cabinet that is not on the list and consider adding it to your kit. Some medicines cannot be left in extreme heat or cold. These should be carried with you, and they can be added to the emergency kit you will be using when you decide to stay or go. Some medicine must be refrigerated. Contact your doctor's office to get ideas on how to best preserve this kind of medicine if you must travel or shelter-in-place without power.

Do you need glasses or contacts? If you do, add a pair of glasses with a recent (if not current) prescription to your emergency travel kit. Include spare contact lenses and solution if you do not have any extra glasses.

Add seasonal items to your emergency travel kit in case you have to leave or abandon your vehicle, or stop and use the vehicle as shelter for an extended period of time. Blankets, gloves, winter boots and hats are critical if you are traveling in areas where there is snow or you expect freezing temperatures. In the summer, include sunscreen and hats to provide protection from the sun.

EMERGENCY SHELTER-IN-PLACE KIT

An emergency can have secondary effects that you can plan for. A tornado can miss your neighborhood but damage the power grid so that you lose power. Your house can sit on high ground but a flood can contaminate your local water supply, so that water must be boiled or treated with chemicals before it is safe to drink.

You may be faced with a loss of power, water and basic community services for days to weeks or longer, depending upon the severity of the emergency. Your emergency shelter-in-place kit is what you will rely on to overcome these losses. This kit is not intended to help you survive for weeks without any assistance from the government. It is intended to help you survive for at least three days while government help is sent to the area and services are being restored.

You should stock your shelter-in-place kit with enough food and water to last at least three days. We recommend one gallon of water per person per day, as well as high-calorie food bars to keep your energy levels up. Canned food and a manual can opener can supplement these food bars. You can also add dehydrated food supplies, but these will require additional water to prepare for meals.

Your emergency shelter-in-place kit should contain a portable weather radio that allows you to follow the emergency and react as needed. This radio should have good batteries, as well as the ability to be charged manually or with a portable solar panel for recharging devices.

If you believe you may have to survive more than three days using your own resources, we recommend adding additional water and food as well as other items to ensure some measure of comfort. See Appendix 1 for sample emergency kit checklists and ideas.

OTHER EMERGENCY KIT CONSIDERATIONS

Whether you stay or evacuate, you will want to provide for any children and pets in your family or group.

Children will need to be distracted from the circumstances of the emergency and may need to be reassured that everything will be fine. Children who are old enough can be included in some of the planning so they understand what you are doing and why. Let them choose several things they would like to include in the travel kit so they can entertain themselves during the journey. Consider including some portable toys or games (including some that do not require power) to entertain children. If you include toys and games as part of your emergency travel kit, avoid things that are bulky, or be prepared to leave them behind if you must abandon your vehicle.

Pets are considered by many people to be part of the family, and mobile pets — like dogs and cats — should be included in planning for an emergency. You will want your emergency kits to include food, water and any medications your pets need. Your "evacuate" option should include identification of vets and veterinary hospitals in cities where you plan on seeking temporary shelter. This is in addition to identification of hospitals, medical centers and specialists to meet the medical needs of you and your family or group.

STAY INFORMED

When you know some kind of emergency is going to happen, or if it is already here, what do you do?

Staying informed is the first action step you take to respond to an actual or potential emergency. You need to get accurate information to start acting on your plans. You will get this information from a number of potential sources. Automated email and text alerts, TV, radio, Twitter, cell phones and local sirens are sources of information. Some can give you specific details about what is happening while others, like sirens, provide you with a warning so you can take cover and seek information from other sources. It is important to make use of multiple sources of information to identify these emergencies and respond based on the planning you already did.

You are now actively checking sources for news on the emergency. This gives you an awareness of the emergency and its secondary effects. Secondary effects include services and travel access we take for granted that could be disrupted by the event that caused the emergency. Flooding could cause an extended loss of power and limit road access to gas stations, grocery stores and hospitals, for example. We will discuss specific emergencies and many of their secondary effects later in this book. We will also talk about how to plan to reduce the impact of the emergency and those effects.

TAKE ACTION

First, do not panic! You have already thought about different emergencies, discussed them with your family or group and prepared to act. If it comes, be calm and follow your plan!

When an emergency is predicted or actually occurs, some people do not respond well to the sudden changes they must make. One of the benefits of your preparations is the time you take to discuss your response to an emergency. As you discuss it, the emergency and the actions you will take to respond to it change it from something that is unknown to something that is closer to ordinary. Remember that people in a group look to the leaders of the group when responding to something like this. If the leaders of a group or family respond with calm and follow the plans already made, others are more likely to follow that example. An adult or older child may need to take extra time to reassure younger children so that others can take the necessary actions to protect everyone.

DECISION: EVACUATE OR SHELTER-IN-PLACE

Make the decision to evacuate or shelter-in-place based on the planning already made for the type of emergency that is predicted or is happening right now. This decision is made by the adults in the family or the group. This is the first real test of a group. Does the group follow a designated leader's decision or a majority vote? If not, then the group can break, with one part evacuating and the other choosing to shelter-in-place. If this happens, their plan is broken and both smaller groups are in greater danger of injury, or worse.

The recommended actions that follow are based on a family or group working together to overcome the challenges of this emergency. While we have Stay Informed, Take Action and Communicate Actions as three separate sections in this chapter, we will be doing all three of them at the same time. If you face an emergency with little to no warning, time will be precious and you will have to act quickly.

ICE: IN CASE OF EMERGENCY

Communicate the decision to shelter-in-place or evacuate. Call and text the local contact and the long-distance contact — "ICE1" and "ICE9" on your cell phone's contact list — with the decision. The long-distance contact should get in touch with each person in the group to let them know whether to stay or leave. This could be calling by phone or, if cell phone and regular phone service are disrupted, sending the information by text message.

Each person should call into their local contact, "ICE1" on your cell phone, to let the local contact know where they are and that they are safe. If they have not already heard from the long-distance contact, the local contact will tell them the decision to stay or leave. If someone is too far away from, or unable to reach, the evacuation point or shelter-in-place location, they need to tell the local and long-distance contacts. These contacts will

let the group know so it is not depending on them or waiting for them to meet at the evacuation point or shelter-in-place location.

One or more adults should go to pick up children and others who have no transportation and bring them back to the location everyone planned to meet at. In your planning, a group should identify one location for the shelter-in-place option and a different location for the evacuate option.

Once everyone is gathered, follow your plan to evacuate or shelter-in-place. Anyone who is not able to reach the location and join you will have to rely on their personal emergency kit and seek shelter nearby, or try to meet you along the evacuation route or at the evacuation destination.

COMMUNICATE ACTIONS

Make sure that the local and long-distance contacts know when everyone is gathered. If some cannot join the main group or family, the long-distance contact should verify where they are and if they are OK. The long-distance contact may be able to direct emergency personnel to a location if needed.

If you evacuate, get in touch with the long-distance contact and let them know who is with you, when you leave and the route you are planning to take to get to your evacuation destination. The long-distance contact can call or text you periodically to let you know the status of the emergency and the status of the route you are trying to use to leave the area. They can also identify potential trouble ahead and redirect you around problem areas. You should communicate regularly until you reach your final evacuation destination. Once you are safe at your new location, get in touch with your long-distance contact and let them know you have arrived.

If you are taking pets with you when you evacuate, remember that most pets are not welcome in public shelters. Consider the arrangements you must make if your evacuation is likely to take more than a day and you will have to rely on public shelters until you can reach your evacuation destination.

If you shelter-in-place, let your local and long-distance contacts know where you are, who is with you and if you have any injuries or medical conditions you cannot treat yourselves. Depending on the severity of the emergency, your contacts may be able to direct emergency aid to your location. You may need to take special precautions to protect yourself based on what caused the emergency. You will respond differently to a tornado than you would to an industrial accident that released a dangerous chemical into the air.

Whether you evacuate or stay, share anything important or unusual about the emergencies with your local and long-distance contacts. This could help save the lives of others and provide the government with information it needs to best respond to an emergency.

YOUR CHECKLIST — PREPARING FOR AN EMERGENCY

Make a Plan

☐ Choose your group;

☐ Discuss your plan with your group or family;

☐ Identify local and long-distance contacts and share plan with them;

☐ Identify where you evacuate to and where you will shelter-in-place;

☐ Agree how you will communicate (do you use Facebook or just phone and text messages, for example);

☐ Finalize your plan and share it with your group as well as your local and long-distance contacts.

Build Your Emergency Kits

☐ Build your emergency travel kit;

☐ Build your emergency shelter-in-place kit.

Stay Informed

☐ Identify a potential emergency or actual emergency;

☐ Start checking TV, radio and the Internet for information;

☐ Decide – is it time for the group to act? If yes – take action.

Take Action

☐ Act on your plan;

☐ Decide — evacuate or shelter-in-place;

☐ Tell the group and your local and long-distance contacts the stay or go decision;

☐ Gather the group;

☐ Load your vehicles to evacuate, or move into your shelter-in-place location:

  ☐ Do you have all your people?

  ☐ Do you have all your pets?

  ☐ Do you have your emergency kit and seasonal supplies (like coats or boots) or shelter-in-place supplies (like plastic and duct tape to seal the room)?

  ☐ Do you have all your prescriptions?

Communicate Actions

❑ If you are evacuating:

  ❑ Get an update from your long-distance contact to see if your evacuation route is still good;

  ❑ Choose your route, communicate it with your contacts and evacuate;

  ❑ Update your contacts with your location as you travel;

  ❑ Let your contacts know when you reach your evacuation location.

❑ If you are going to shelter-in-place:

  ❑ Take precautions based on the emergency you face;

  ❑ Seal the room with plastic and duct tape if there is contaminated air;

  ❑ Communicate with your contacts until the emergency has ended.

Notes

Notes

Notes

Chapter 2:
Primary Disaster Effects

SCAN FOR CHAPTER
OVERVIEW VIDEO

Disasters, whether natural or man-made, create emergencies. To prepare for these emergencies, we must understand the dangers we will face, and how to overcome them.

In Chapter 1, you learned how to plan for an emergency and how to decide whether to evacuate or shelter-in-place based on the situation. Your ability to take care of yourself and others is significantly improved because you planned ahead.

The next step is to learn what to do during the emergency. What should you expect and do if you are sheltering-in-place during a tornado or earthquake? What should you expect and do if you are evacuating an area threatened by a hurricane or flood? How do you protect yourself and others?

Disasters can cause injury and property damage in many ways. To keep things simple, we break them down into primary disaster effects and secondary disaster effects. Primary effects impact you right now — the wind from a tornado or the water from flooding. Secondary effects will influence you later and longer — the loss of electricity from downed power lines, or the loss of access to your hospital and grocery store because flood waters washed out the road.

This chapter will focus on primary disaster effects: how to prepare for them, and how to protect yourself and others from them. Chapter 3 will focus on secondary disaster effects with the same goals: prepare and protect. Chapters 4 through 13 will talk about specific types of disasters, and the special considerations for each type of event that could impact your emergency planning and your options to evacuate or shelter-in-place.

PRIMARY EFFECTS

Primary disaster effects will impact your ability to evacuate the area or to shelter-in-place. You can prepare for them, and you can seek protection from them, but these effects can only be avoided if you evacuate ahead of the disaster. Sudden disasters, like a tornado or an industrial accident, can cause an emergency with effects that you cannot escape. Whether you cannot evacuate the area before a disaster or it strikes with no warning, you will need to learn how to prepare and protect from primary disaster effects.

There are general prepare-action steps you should always take, regardless of the emergencies you may face.

Plan ahead and build your emergency kits, using the equipment and supply checklists in Appendix 1, starting on page 214. What else should you do to prepare?

MAINTAIN EVACUATION VEHICLE(S)

Always keep at least half a tank of gas in your vehicle(s), because you may not have time to gas up when the emergency comes.

Rotate your tires when you change the oil, and replace your tires when they are worn. They are a weak link when evacuating, and tire problems that stop you while you are on the road during an emergency put you and others at risk.

If your car is prone to breakdowns, plan alternate travel arrangements now, before an emergency occurs.

Keep a complete emergency travel kit in your evacuation vehicle(s). Update this kit with seasonal clothing and supplies, like sunscreen, as you head into winter and summer. Consider updating your emergency travel kit with these items when you change your clocks to and from Daylight Savings Time. The key is to make sure you always update your emergency travel kit!

MAINTAIN SHELTER-IN-PLACE LOCATION

Have your furnace and air-conditioning system checked every year. When extreme heat or cold arrives, you do not want to have to evacuate into an emergency that puts you and others at greater risk.

Keep the interior room or place where you will seek shelter free from clutter. You and your family or group needs to be able to safely move into and shelter there with little warning, and by flashlight if the power is out.

Keep several flashlights in different parts of the house or place you live, including one you can find quickly. At night, with no power, a flashlight will reduce the chance of injury and help young children control their fear in what may be a scary situation. Consider keeping at least one manual flashlight on hand where you live so you have a light source that does not depend on power or batteries.

Store your emergency shelter-in-place kit where you will shelter or very close to your shelter-in-place location. Replace any items, particularly food and medical supplies, that may be taken from the kit for daily use. If possible, do not rely on any emergency kit for batteries, food or other supplies.

You have now prepared for disasters ahead of time. But when a disaster comes, you will still need to protect yourself and others from primary disaster effects.

Each disaster can create an emergency with effects that vary across the disaster area. A thunderstorm can deliver heavy rain in one place and barely wet the ground somewhere else.

Some disasters can combine the effects of other disasters, creating additional effects that are even more dangerous. A wind storm, for example, has one set of effects while a heavy thunderstorm typically has a different set of effects. When you have a hurricane with both high winds and heavy rains, you get the effects you would expect from wind and rain, but you also get additional effects unique to a hurricane.

Now, let's discuss primary disaster effects. We will do this based on how they will affect us versus focusing on each individual disaster effect. To do this, we will group primary disaster effects into five categories: Air, Water, Earth, Fire and Other. Each category will highlight disasters and related effects. Each category will also include your considerations to prepare and protect from those effects. Some of the effects could be common to several categories but they will only be listed once, with specific prepare-and-protect guidance found in that category.

AIR

Air may seem like it should be the least of the effects we worry about, since we don't normally see it, and it weighs nothing. Air is really like an ocean that surrounds us. There are currents of air constantly moving, with warm air rising and cool air falling. Air carries moisture that can become rain or snow depending on the temperature. The direction and speed at which air moves, the amount of moisture it carries and changes in temperature are the leading reasons for disasters caused by air. When two air masses collide, we can get thunderstorms, tornadoes, snow, a hail storm or even an ice storm.

Air effects are caused by disasters like tornadoes, extreme winter storms, blizzards, ice storms, wind storms and intense cold. Air effects include flying debris, destructive high winds, lightning strikes, reduced visibility, extreme cold and drifting snow.

PREPARE

The air category involves temperature, wind speed and can include rain or snow. This is one of three weather-related categories.

You and your family or group should prepare by learning about and discussing the different air emergencies and how to protect from their effects. Add seasonal items to your emergency kits. In winter, add heavy clothing and blankets to your emergency travel kit, and in summer, add hats and sunscreen. You may not need to add these supplies to your shelter-in-place kit unless you are sheltering away from your home or shelter location and will not have access to your seasonal clothing.

PROTECT — STAY INFORMED

Some air disasters, like tornadoes, come suddenly. If you are not near a TV or radio, you may only have sirens to warn you. As soon as you hear sirens, check at least one other source for news. You need to know what is happening so that you can decide what actions to take.

When the National Weather Service declares a Watch, an Advisory or a Warning, what is the difference? A Watch (a Tornado or Winter Storm Watch, for example) means the conditions can produce the named weather event, and it could impact you. An Advisory (a Freezing Rain Advisory or a Wind Advisory, for example) means there is a reasonable chance that the named weather event will occur, and it is likely to impact you. A Warning (a Tornado Warning or Blizzard Warning, for example) means the named weather event is happening, and you may be in its path.

Some weather events, like a tornado, are short-lived and only affect a small area within a much larger weather event, like a series of thunderstorms. Tornadoes can, however, cause great destruction, injury and even loss of life in that small area. Other weather events, like a blizzard, can cover a much larger area and last for many hours, but they are usually less destructive and they injure or kill because of long exposure to an effect, like extreme cold.

SEEK SHELTER

A shelter can protect you from many of the effects of air-category disasters. Tornadoes can pick up debris and hurl it through the air at high speeds. Wind storms can do the same.

If you have time to close window shutters or put plywood over windows, this can reduce the chance that small flying debris will break them and shower you with broken glass. Blizzards can bring significant snowfall with drifting and extreme cold. You have chosen your shelter-in-place location carefully and have your complete emergency shelter-in-place kit with you.

We will discuss shelter-in-place considerations for specific types of disasters in chapters 4 through 13. You may have to choose several shelter-in-place options based on the type of disaster that occurs. A mobile home, for example, can shelter you from a blizzard but it is not where you want to shelter from a tornado.

Communicate

Keep your local and long-distance contacts informed about your safety and situation. If someone is badly injured, tell your contacts and try to arrange for medical treatment. Once the emergency is past, make sure any injuries are evaluated and treated by medical professionals.

WATER

Water effects are everywhere, and usually go unnoticed.

A single raindrop can cause a tiny amount of erosion, streams and rivers slowly erode their banks, and ocean waves erode beaches. Water effects can become dangerous when they overwhelm the ability of the land to absorb them or they surge beyond riverbanks and beaches. Thunderstorms and hurricanes can cause rain to fall so quickly that it cannot be absorbed by the soil. It overwhelms storm drain systems and it causes streams and rivers to overflow their banks. When this happens, flash floods and flooding can occur, washing out roads and covering highways and homes. A tsunami can be even worse, sending a wall of water traveling at the speed of a train across miles of land. This can lead to a significant loss of life and great destruction.

Water effects are caused by disasters such as hurricanes, tsunami, heavy rain and snow. Water effects include flooding, flash floods, storm surge, riptides and ice.

PREPARE

The water category involves water from rain, storm surge and snowmelt, as well as rivers, lakes and oceans. This is the second of three weather-related categories.

You and your family or group should prepare by learning about and discussing the different water emergencies and how to protect from their effects. You also need to discuss the strengths and weaknesses of your shelter-in-place location. It may be fine when you are facing rain and wind from a heavy thunderstorm or a category 1 hurricane, but the wind and water effects from a category 4 or 5 hurricane are much more dangerous and could overwhelm your shelter's ability to protect you and others.

If you are not sure your shelter will withstand certain disasters, plan to evacuate. In the event you will not have time to evacuate, you should plan on using a stronger shelter-in-place location. Check with your city or county officials about the location of an alternate shelter-in-place location that is better suited to shelter people in more dangerous weather event emergencies. If you are in a tsunami zone or live on a coast, you should plan to evacuate if there is a tsunami warning or an event that could cause a tsunami, like an earthquake offshore. Chapter 10 will cover how to prepare and protect from a tsunami in greater detail.

PROTECT — STAY INFORMED

You may receive warnings well before some water disasters, like a hurricane, occur. Authorities, however, may not know where the worst part of the disaster will strike. Other water disasters, like flash floods and tsunami, come suddenly. If you are not near a TV or radio, you may only have sirens to warn you. As soon as you hear sirens, check at least one other source for news. You need to know what is happening so that you can decide what actions to take.

The National Weather Service will issue Watches, Advisories and Warnings for most water effects. Remember that these go from the least dangerous, a Watch, to the most dangerous, a Warning.

SEEK SHELTER

Do you live in a flood zone, near a stream or river, or on a coast? If you do, you are more likely to face flooding.

Use history as a guide but be prepared for surprises. The history books may show that the river you live near has never risen to the height of your shelter-in-place location. This is no guarantee that the river will not rise higher and flood your shelter location, only that it is not likely or has not happened since people started keeping track of disasters where you live. Whether you are facing a flood or a tsunami, shelter may change to any higher ground. This could mean moving into the hills, going up to a higher floor in a tall building or getting on the roof where you live. A sudden rise in water may not give you time to evacuate away from the water, but only to evacuate upward.

COMMUNICATE

Keep your local and long-distance contacts informed about your safety and situation. If you or someone in your group is badly injured, tell your contacts and try to arrange for medical treatment.

If you are stranded in a location surrounded by water, find a way to keep your cell phone dry so that you can call for help once the worst of the disaster is behind you. A thick, waterproof and airtight bag will keep your cell phone dry until you need it. Once the emergency is past, make sure any injuries are evaluated and treated by medical professionals.

EARTH

We live, work and build on solid ground. It represents security and we trust it to stay put. The sudden movement of earth, whether from an earthquake, volcano or landslide, can put us at great risk.

Some earth disasters, like a landslide, cover a small area and have no primary disaster effect outside the location of the landslide. Other earth disasters, like an earthquake, have primary disaster effects that can occur hundreds of miles from the location of the earthquake. These effects, like building damage and destruction, can lead to many injuries and

major loss of life. Earthquakes often occur when volcanoes erupt, and they are one of the disasters that can cause tsunamis. Earthquakes will be discussed in greater detail later in this book.

Earth effects are caused by disasters such as earthquakes, mudslides, landslides and sinkholes. Earth effects include destruction to buildings, roads and bridges, shaking and movement of the earth, as well as fire.

PREPARE

The earth category involves sudden vertical and horizontal movement of the ground, shaking of the ground and nearby structures, and collapse of areas and buildings that have become unstable.

You and your family or group should prepare by learning about and discussing the different earth emergencies and how to protect from their effects. Your preparations for a landslide are different than those for an earthquake. Landslides and sinkholes are local events, while earthquakes can impact a broader area.

A good way to avoid landslides is to avoid building your house on steep slopes or existing landslides. If you are uncertain about how stable your home or shelter-in-place location is, consider paying an expert, like a civil engineer, to evaluate the location and propose ways to stabilize your foundation if problems are noted.

Earthquakes are not just something that people from California need to plan for. There are fault lines — areas in the earth where stress builds up — that can shift suddenly to release that stress. This release results in movement of the ground and can occur without much warning. Choose your shelter-in-place building for its ability to withstand the impact of an earthquake. Prepare your shelter-in-place location within the building so that heavy objects are close to the floor and pictures and other wall hangings are not positioned over your seats. If possible, add a piece of sturdy furniture, like a table, that you can shelter under to protect from falling debris and objects.

PROTECT — STAY INFORMED

Some earth disasters will come with little to no warning. A series of small tremors can happen repeatedly without being followed by a large earthquake. Then one day, the tremors occur, and shortly thereafter, a large earthquake follows.

There is no accurate earthquake prediction system, so your first warning may be the start of a large earthquake shaking your location. You have to decide when the tremors and earth movement are dangerous enough for you to shelter-in-place.

Stay tuned to a TV or radio so you are aware of other effects that can create additional danger. If there was, for example, a large offshore earthquake that occurred when quake effects struck your area, you may have to prepare for a tsunami soon after the earthquake stops.

SEEK SHELTER

Move to your shelter-in-place location and take shelter, preferably under a sturdy piece of furniture, like a table. You may need to put on dust masks or put a piece of cloth over your mouth to help you breathe. Do not leave your shelter until you believe the earthquake is over. There may be sizeable aftershocks after the large earthquake and these could cause additional debris or even parts of the building to fall or collapse.

COMMUNICATE

Keep your local and long-distance contacts informed about your safety and situation. If you or someone in your group is badly injured, tell your contacts and try to arrange for medical treatment. Once the emergency is past, make sure any injuries are evaluated and treated by medical professionals.

Earthquakes damage and destroy buildings, roads and bridges, so you may have to take care of yourself and others for more than three days before any meaningful help can reach you. If your shelter is badly damaged and you cannot stay there safely, it may also be difficult to leave the area and find new shelter.

FIRE

Fire effects — where we can control them — are something we rely on for comfort, food and even clean water. We need a working furnace to heat our homes. Our vehicle's heater keeps us warm during the cold winter months. And fire, whether from an electric stove, gas flame or wood, allows us to cook food and boil water.

Fire effects — when uncontrolled — can be very dangerous. They can spread and grow quickly, and it may be difficult or even impossible to shelter-in-place from some of these effects. Some fire effects, like lava, cover small areas and, with warning, can be avoided. Many fire effects can combine with air effects to spread over larger areas. Poisonous gas release and ash clouds from a volcano as well as fires from wildfires can be much harder to avoid. Too much heat or smoke can injure or kill if you cannot escape these effects.

Fire effects are caused by disasters like volcanoes, wildfires and heat waves. Fire effects include lava flows, poisonous gas release, ash clouds, fire storms, smoke and extreme heat.

PREPARE

The fire category involves heat, smoke and different types of fires. This is the last of three weather-related categories.

You and your family or group should prepare by learning about and discussing the different fire emergencies and how to protect from their effects. There is only one effect that involves your shelter-in-place option — a heat wave. You must find a way to stay cool.

This starts with making sure your air-conditioning unit is well maintained. You can also buy several fans and prepare a living space in the coolest area where you live.

Other fire effects will likely give you no option but to evacuate. Find out how your community and county provide warnings about volcano and fire effects. Sign up for an alert service so that you receive a text message or email when an alert is sent. If you live in an area prone to volcanic activity or you have had a very dry summer creating conditions perfect for fires, your best "prepare" action is to maintain your vehicle so you can evacuate quickly. A volcano can erupt and you may have some warning time to evacuate. Wildfires can start with a lightning strike, hot ash or cinders from a volcano, human carelessness or even arson. You may have warning time to evacuate or simply see a large smoke cloud out your window. Be prepared to leave quickly.

PROTECT — STAY INFORMED

Fire effects can occur suddenly and move quickly. Smoke and ash can be carried by high winds to cover a large area. Sirens could warn you that there is danger, but this is not guaranteed. Rely on multiple sources of information so you know what is happening and can react as needed. Remember to look for an alert message from the service you joined as well as checking TV and radio.

SEEK SHELTER

Seek shelter from a heat wave. Bring extra water into the living space you prepared in the coolest part of the house. Shelter here as needed if you lose power or have air-conditioning problems.

Evacuate away from lava, fires and other volcano and wildfire effects. Distance is your best shelter, and your evacuation vehicle is key to getting you and others away from the disaster effects. Lava and heavy ash clouds will flow and move downhill. Try to evacuate by moving away from the paths these effects will follow. If you have to evacuate while ash is falling, your car engine could stall if your air filter gets clogged. If you must abandon your vehicle, you will need to use masks, long-sleeve shirts or jackets and hats to try to protect from falling ash. Head to higher ground and seek shelter only if you cannot evacuate away from these kinds of effects. Additional guidance is found in later chapters that cover wildfires and volcanoes.

COMMUNICATE

Keep your local and long-distance contacts informed about your safety and situation. If you are unable to evacuate or you lose your transportation and are on foot, let your contacts know and they may be able to help you reach emergency personnel who can provide evacuation assistance. If anyone is badly injured, tell your contacts and try to arrange for medical treatment.

When you are evacuating away from fire effects, you may only have time for the most serious treatments — starting breathing and stopping bleeding — before you continue to evacuate. Once the emergency is past or you are no longer in the emergency area, make sure any injuries are evaluated and treated by medical professionals.

OTHER

"Other" is the final disaster category and includes primarily events that are related to human accidents or criminal choice. This category also includes epidemics, like the flu that hits every fall, which can occur naturally. We rely on the tools of a modern society to make a good living for ourselves and our family and friends. These same tools can break, creating an industrial accident, or be turned against people for some political purpose, like a terrorist attack. Whether a chemical release, for example, was an accident or part of a criminal plan like a terrorist attack, you have to prepare and protect from the effects.

Other effects can be caused by epidemics, industrial accidents and terrorist attacks. This category includes man-caused disasters. Examples of "other" disasters include: the H1N1 (flu) pandemic scare, the Fukushima Daiichi nuclear disaster following the 2011 tsunami that hit Japan's East coast, and the infamous Sept. 11, 2001, terrorist attack that destroyed the twin towers of the World Trade Center in New York City.

Other effects can include the following and more: disease outbreak, damage and destruction of buildings, the spread of radiation from a nuclear reactor meltdown or from a terrorist use of a nuclear device, and the spread of a poisonous liquid or gas from an industrial accident.

PREPARE

This category involves different types of effects. How do you prepare for them? We talked about important prepare work you can do to get ready for any emergency effect: plan, build your emergencies kits, and maintain your evacuation vehicle(s) and shelter-in-place location.

Are any of these effects like the air, water, earth and fire effects we talked about earlier in this chapter? If the effects are the same or similar to an effect we have talked about, you

already know how to prepare and protect from that effect. For example, if the effect is moving fire, you would treat it like a wildfire and evacuate away from it. If the effect is a gas cloud, you would treat it as if it was from a volcano, and evacuate away and upwind from it. The safety of you and others depends on how well you prepare for and protect from an effect.

A disease outbreak usually happens when a disease starts to spread because our bodies cannot fight it. This becomes more dangerous when the disease spreads easily from person to person. If the disease spreads out over a large area, it may be called an epidemic. A pandemic is an epidemic that has spread out over several continents. If there are warnings about an epidemic or a pandemic, you may want to buy enough food for weeks, so you can avoid going to the grocery store. The key with diseases that are spread from person to person is to limit the number of people you see. This will reduce the chance that you or someone in your family or group will get the disease. Chapter 11 will provide more information about actions to prepare and protect from a disease outbreak or epidemic.

PROTECT — STAY INFORMED

You might hear a siren or something on the TV or radio telling you about a terrorist attack or a bad industrial accident that has just occurred. Take time to find out what has actually happened. A terrorist attack or an industrial accident is horrible but you need to know what the effects are before you can decide to evacuate or shelter-in-place. Gather information to make your decision.

SEEK SHELTER

When the effect you are protecting yourself from is a disease that spreads easily from person to person, like the flu, you should shelter-in-place. Avoid meeting others who could give you the disease. This could include working from home, keeping children home from school, and avoiding church gatherings and trips to the mall, for example. If a family or group member becomes sick, only one other person in the group should care for the sick person. The sick person should have their own room and they should not spend time with the rest of the group until they no longer spread the disease. Chapter 11 will provide more detail on how to protect a family or group from an epidemic.

You should evacuate away from effects that are mobile, like a moving fire or gas cloud, or from effects that will hurt you through time, like radiation from a reactor leak or a terrorist attack.

COMMUNICATE

Keep your local and long-distance contacts informed about your safety and situation. If you will have to evacuate into a danger area, your contacts may be able to tell you the safest route for you to get through the area quickly.

If you or someone in your group is badly injured or sick, tell your contacts and try to arrange for medical treatment. In the case of an epidemic, the U.S. Postal Service may be able to deliver drugs to help those who are sick. If the authorities are going to deliver medicine this way, they will give instructions on TV and the radio so that everyone knows what to do. Follow those instructions.

Once an epidemic emergency is past, make sure any sick and injured are evaluated and treated by medical professionals.

There may be primary effects that are not mentioned in this chapter. If the effect is not mentioned above, which category has effects like it? Try to match these effects to one of the categories we discussed, and then follow your prepare and protect guidance for that category.

CONCLUSION

In this chapter, we have talked about disaster effects that are frightening. Fear and confusion are natural when an emergency happens. The planning and discussions you have before an emergency should reduce the fear and confusion for your family or group. When an emergency happens, some adults as well as children will still need coaching to help them stay focused on action and not give in to fear.

YOUR CHECKLIST —
PRIMARY DISASTER EFFECTS

Prepare For Primary Disaster Effects

Build Your Emergency Kits

Make a Plan

Maintain Your Evacuation Vehicle(s)

❑ Keep your car at half a tank of gas or more;
❑ Take care of good tires, replace worn tires;
❑ Plan alternate travel arrangements in case of breakdown;
❑ Update your emergency travel kit with seasonal clothing and items.

Maintain Your Shelter-In-Place Location

❑ Inspect your furnace and air-conditioning systems, repair if needed;
❑ Keep your shelter-in-place location free from clutter;
❑ Put flashlights where they are easy to reach if needed;
❑ Buy at least one manual flashlight for your shelter location;
❑ Store your emergency shelter-in-place kit in or near where you will shelter.

Protect From Primary Disaster Effects

❑ Evacuate – decide to leave or stay;
❑ Shelter-in-place:
    ❑ Stay Informed using contacts, phone, TV and radio;
    ❑ Seek Shelter based on the primary disaster effects identified;
    ❑ Communicate with local and long-distance contacts.

In general:

❑ *Evacuate* from effects that are mobile, like fire or poisonous gas clouds, or that can hurt you through time, like radiation exposure.
❑ *Seek shelter* from effects that are not likely to seriously damage or destroy your shelter location, like a blizzard or heat wave.

Notes

Notes

Notes

Chapter 3:
Secondary Disaster Effects

SCAN FOR CHAPTER OVERVIEW VIDEO

When a disaster strikes, you act on your planning, and protect yourself and others from the effects of the event. But the struggle to get back to normal does not end when the disaster is over. It may have even created other problems you have to overcome.

In Chapter 2, we talked about the effects of disasters and divided them into two broad groups: primary effects and secondary effects. Chapter 2 discussed primary effects that impact you during the emergency, and how to prepare and protect from these effects. This chapter will talk about secondary effects, and how to prepare for and overcome them. These effects impact you through time, like the loss of power or the loss of access to your hospital and grocery store because of damage.

Secondary effects can last far longer than the emergency that created them. The impact can vary from large to small, changing with the season and the length of time you lose access to something you rely on. The loss of power for a week during an extremely cold winter could be very dangerous, while finding one of many nearby gas stations closed due to storm damage is probably just a small problem.

SECONDARY EFFECTS

In Chapter 2, you learned to stay informed, protect and communicate before and during a disaster. Communication does not stop with the end of primary disaster effects. If you evacuated before or during the disaster, you need to know if it is safe to return to your home. If you sheltered-in-place, you need to know if you can safely stay in your shelter. Talk to contacts and friends who stayed in the disaster area. Check with the authorities, and follow TV and Internet updates, as well as radio broadcasts. Can you safely return or stay? How badly was your area and your home affected by secondary disaster effects?

These are effects that can last for days, months or even years. They are part of the aftermath of any disaster. Effects from a small flood might be cleaned up and repaired quickly once a river is no longer above flood stage. A large hurricane, like Katrina, could cause damage that takes years to fix. What do you do if your house is badly damaged or you have no power or running water? Have emergency services — like police, fire and medical — been restored in your area? These are some of the secondary effects that you may have to overcome once the disaster is over. How do you prepare and protect from these effects?

Let's talk about secondary disaster effects. What should you be concerned about? Is it more important to protect from some effects than from others? These effects involve the loss of many services and capabilities that we rely on for our long-term health and survival. This loss means that some of our needs are no longer being met. The questions you should ask are: if I lose this service, what will I do? Can you and others survive if this need is not met? These services and needs can be grouped into several categories, as follows:

- Essential for long-term health and survival: emergency room services, power, water, food, shelter, communication;
- Very important for long-term health and survival: emergency services (police, fire, ambulance), transportation (your vehicle and mass transit), access to fuel, roads, medicine;
- Important for long-term health and survival: hospital, postal, school, veterinary, animal control, garbage services.

Some of these services and needs can vary in their importance depending upon other factors. These factors include: the time of year of the disaster; how large an area has been deprived of certain services and capabilities; and how long they will not be available. You might be able to shelter in a house missing most of its roof during late summer or early fall, but this shelter is probably not enough to protect you from the effects of extreme cold and snow if it was all you had for weeks in January.

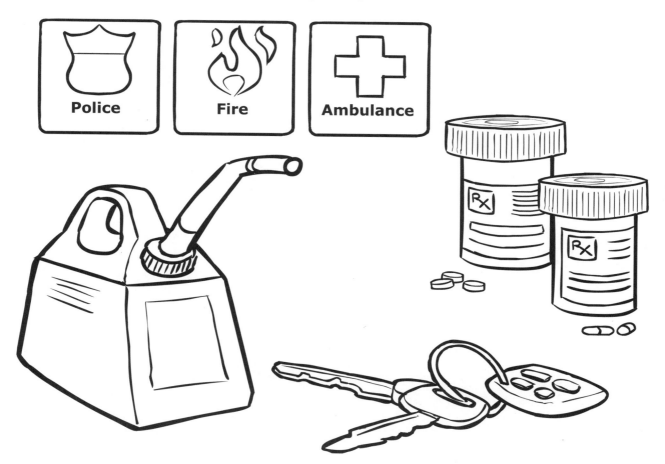

ESSENTIAL SERVICES & NEEDS
EMERGENCY ROOM SERVICES

Emergency room services will be needed when you or someone in your family or group has a life-threatening injury. This need might come during the disaster or after it is past. This could involve life-saving first aid that someone in the group will have to perform, especially if an ambulance cannot reach you in time.

Action Steps:

- Treat seriously injured people first, and remember: start breathing, stop bleeding. Treat for shock if needed. To learn more about how to perform first aid like this, go to www.redcross.org to learn before a disaster strikes.
- Call for medical assistance. Use your local and long-distance contacts to help if you are not able to request medical help directly.

    If medical help cannot be sent to you, can the seriously injured person be moved safely? Find out if it is safe enough for someone in your group to take anyone with serious injuries and drive them to a hospital or doctor's office. If it safe enough, take seriously injured people to get medical help. Before sending someone out to try to reach a hospital during a disaster, make sure the injury is worth the risk. Once the driver and one or several injured leave, they will be at greater risk and separated from the rest of the group.
- Treat minor injuries. When the disaster is over and you can safely reach a hospital or doctor's office, take any injured for an evaluation and any needed treatment. This is particularly important for the very young and old.

POWER

We take it for granted — when you flip on the light switch, you expect it to work. If nothing happens, you check your fuse box or a circuit breaker, but what if you can't see a problem? Then you call the power company and tell them about the power problem and ask when it will be restored. When a disaster knocks out your power, you have lost an essential service that you rely on. It can heat and cool your home, run your refrigerator and stove, and provide light during any conditions. Outside your home, it is critical to the services you rely on. Hospitals, grocery stores, gas stations and cell phone towers all require power to work.

If you lose power because of a disaster, you need to know how long the power company says it will take for power to be restored. You also need to know where to go to get access to power. Some disasters, like a large windstorm, can knock out power across several states and put half a million people in the dark. Most of the people and businesses in those states will still have power. You might have to drive a few miles to get to a restaurant, for example, but once there, you may be able to charge your phone, check the Internet and TV for news, and get a hot meal. This means that you have access to power even if your home does not. You might not have hot water for a shower and have to eat cold meals or grill more often, but this more nuisance than danger. In a windstorm like this, for example, power might take three to seven days to be restored. If power is the only essential service you lost and you still have access to power nearby, you can still return home or stay at home.

Few disasters are so destructive and widespread that they cause the loss of power everywhere for hundreds of miles in all directions. If this happens, it could take a number of weeks or longer to restore power throughout the area. An extended period without power — weeks or longer — will shut down everything that does not have an alternate power source like an emergency generator. This is a much more dangerous situation. Priorities will go to keep hospitals up and running, with the possibility they will have to be evacuated if they cannot continue to take care of their patients. The authorities will probably push to evacuate everyone who is still present in the disaster area.

If you lose power for a short time, three to seven days, how do you prepare and protect?

Prepare:

- Stock up on additional firewood, charcoal or propane for a grill to cook hot meals.
- Buy a solar-powered charger to recharge portable devices like your cell phone. Your cell phone will function normally unless the disaster did major damage to the network of cell towers that support cell phone communications. Satellite phones will work in an area where cell phones do not. If this capability is important to you, then consider buying a satellite phone.
- Do you have a family or group member who requires life-saving medicine that must be kept cold? This would be a good reason to buy an emergency generator. This generator would not be able to provide power for everything in the house, but it could provide power to a refrigerator and charge portable devices like cell phones. If you buy a generator, it will probably run on a fuel like gasoline or diesel, so you will have to store or buy extra fuel. If the disaster is bad enough, you may not be able to get more fuel once you run out of what you have on hand.

Protect:

- Keep your cell phone charged. Use the solar charging device to recharge your cell phones and radios. Stay in touch with your local and long-distance contacts and listen for guidance from the authorities. Limit driving until you are able to find gas and refuel.
- Cook all the meat in your refrigerator and freezer before it goes bad. Perhaps you can have a neighborhood cookout or just a backyard barbeque for your family or group. You made it through the disaster, so celebrate and try to keep your spirits up. Save canned and boxed food for later. Try to have at least one hot meal a day, especially if it is cold outside. Do not use a propane grill inside, or run a generator inside. They should only be used outside where there is good ventilation. They give off carbon monoxide, which can be deadly. The Center for Disease Control (CDC) estimates that carbon monoxide poisoning kills almost 500 people per year.
- Talk to children about the disaster. Treat recovering from it like an adventure and they may start treating it the same way. Create some routines to help children adapt to the loss of power. These can include activities like reading together for an hour, playing a board game, and going to bed at the same time as normal and in their own beds, if possible. Your calm response will reassure the children and help them believe that things will be OK.

If you lose power for a long time, weeks or more, how do you prepare and protect?

You have to decide whether you need to evacuate or not. In spring, summer or fall, the loss of power by itself may not threaten injury or worse. In winter, with no heat in the house and no way to know when power will return, your only choice may be to evacuate. How far do you need to travel to get access to power for water, groceries, gas, medicine and a hospital? If you are on the edge of a large disaster area or the disaster affected a small area, then you may be able to shelter-in-place. You will have to travel to get what you need and wait until power is restored.

You prepare when you plan to evacuate if the effects of the disaster are too much to overcome. If you are in the middle of a large disaster area and there is no power for a hundred miles or more in any direction, staying becomes much more dangerous than evacuating.

You protect by learning about the situation from your contacts and the authorities. You discuss your options and you decide whether or not you can safely stay. You take the best option for you and others based on your situation and the secondary disaster effects you face. In this case, you evacuate.

WATER, FOOD, SHELTER & COMMUNICATION

You need water, food, shelter and the ability to communicate. If you lose access to any of these essential services or needs, your long-term health will suffer and your chances of survival could be reduced. The longer you must go without one or more of these — particularly water, food and shelter — the more danger you are in. How do you prepare and protect from the loss of these essentials for a short time, like three to seven days, or for a period of weeks and longer?

Prepare — 3–7 days

- You already started to prepare for disasters when you built an emergency shelter-in-place kit with enough food and water to last at least three days. You can add extra food and water to your shelter-in-place kit to last seven days or more. You also bought a solar charger to power your cell phone. Buy a portable water filter. You can use this to purify water, including snowmelt, that has not been properly treated for drinking. You need to check your home or the location where you sheltered-in-place. Was it badly damaged by primary disaster effects, like high winds or flood waters? If it was not badly damaged, then you can return home or continue to stay at your shelter-in-place location. If it was badly damaged, is it still safe to stay there? If it is not, you need to evacuate.

Protect — 3–7 days

- Stay informed. Talk to your contacts, use the Internet, and listen to the authorities so you know where you can get water, food and access to power to recharge your cell phone. This is an alternative if you do not have a solar charger or cannot charge your phone using a car adapter.
- Take action. Restock your water and food after the primary disaster effects are over. Recharge your cell phone and get gas. If these essential services are not available nearby, you will have to decide if you need to evacuate. Your preparations will help determine if you can safely stay. Do you have enough food and water to last until the authorities say they can bring more in? If you cannot restock your food and water and it will run out before help arrives, then you need to evacuate.
- Communicate. Stay in touch with your contacts. Share information with local contacts about locations with water, food or gas. Tell your long-distance contacts that

you made it through the disaster. You may need to send some children to stay with family or friends outside the disaster area while the adults repair the home and make it safe to live in. Tell the authorities about effects, and people, that cause dangers in the disaster area.

Prepare — weeks or longer

- You talked about what you would do with your family or group. If you lose access to water, food, shelter or the ability to communicate for weeks or more, the only safe option is to evacuate. If you lose access to water and food, in particular, you must leave and move toward a part of the region that can still offer these. Water is the most important of these four essential services and needs. Use your portable water filter to purify water so you do not run out while you evacuate.

Protect — weeks or longer

- Stay informed. Talk to your contacts, use the Internet and listen to the authorities so you know the best way to evacuate from the area. If your home is fine but there is no drinking water, food or power for heating and cooking, your long-term health and safety will be at risk if you stay.
- Take action. You need to act when your health and safety are at risk. Evacuate just like you would if you had warning that a deadly disaster was coming. In this case, you are evacuating away from the loss of essential services and needs that cannot be met. Bring extra water and food. You are evacuating through a large disaster area and it may take days to drive a few hundred miles to safety.
- Communicate. Stay in touch with your contacts. Share information with local contacts about the best way to evacuate the area. Talk with your long-distance contacts and ask their help with the evacuation route once you leave the local area. Your long-distance contacts can check with the authorities and help guide you. This allows you to focus on evacuating and avoiding any dangers you encounter while traveling through the disaster area. Share information on the safety of roads and bridges with the authorities and your contacts so that others can avoid hazards you discover.

VERY IMPORTANT SERVICES & NEEDS

These services and needs are very important for long-term health and survival. They include: emergency services (police, fire and ambulance), transportation (your vehicle and mass transit), and access to fuel, roads and medicine.

Emergency services are not something you need every hour. They are needed when something goes wrong. They also provide you with a sense of safety. The fire department can respond to put out a fire or stop it from spreading, while an ambulance can reach you quickly to help with a serious injury. These services help treat personal tragedies, your injury or a fire in your home, for example.

Emergency services can also help us limit the spread of personal tragedies and reduce the chance that they will create a larger disaster. A house fire in a crowded neighborhood

could grow and burn through the whole neighborhood and beyond without a quick or large enough fire service response. The Great Chicago Fire of 1871 was thought to have started in a small barn in a crowded neighborhood. It lasted for two days, burning through several square miles of central Chicago. By the time rain put it out, several hundred people had died and almost 100,000 people were left homeless. A large disaster could leave part of the disaster area with less fire service than Chicago had more than 140 years ago.

Other very important services and needs include transportation, fuel, roads and medicine. These services assist with movement — your ability to travel to meet your needs and the ability of service providers and disaster assistance personnel to reach you. These services enable you and others to travel for essential services and meet essential needs. They include the ability to get and renew prescriptions you need for your long-term health. They are very important to your long-term health and significantly improve your ability to survive after a disaster has passed. While these services are not as critical as power, water and food, their loss will still put you in danger. How do you prepare and protect from the loss of these services?

Prepare

- Let's start with emergency services. Municipal police, fire and ambulance services are here to protect, keep order and provide different kinds of assistance. You cannot replace all these services with the limited number of people and skills in your family or group, so do not try to. Focus on what you can do, for example: keep an extra fire extinguisher in your house, one in each vehicle and at least one in your shelter-in-place location; take a first-aid class so you can perform life-saving first aid and better treat other injuries; notify the authorities if you see any looting or violence.

- Transportation, fuel and roads are vital to the movement of people and services. They make it easier for you to go get more food, water and medicine as well as giving emergency services access to help. You can overcome some of the effects of this loss by preparing ahead of the disaster. Take good care of your vehicle(s) and tires. Always keep at least half a tank of gas in your vehicle(s).

  Store a good pair of walking shoes in your shelter-in-place location just in case walking is your only option once a disaster is over. It's also a good idea to have a good pair of walking shoes with you where you work. Some shoes, like business shoes, are not intended for a comfortable walk of miles. Sandals and flip-flops might be comfortable, but you would not want to walk across broken glass and debris with nails if you had a choice. Pick practical shoes or boots that will protect your feet.

  Some families like to ride bikes. If you cannot evacuate with a vehicle, bikes may be able to help. One or two bike riders can also help a larger walking group find a way through a badly damaged area to get to safety.

If you have a four-wheel-drive vehicle, count yourself lucky. This vehicle will be better able to move through much of the damage that would stop other vehicles.

- The best way to prepare for the shortage of an important medicine is to get an extra prescription filled ahead of any disaster. If your doctor cannot give you an extra prescription, ask what other non-prescription medications you can buy to use in place of the prescription if there is an emergency.

Protect

- Stay informed. Talk to your contacts, use the Internet, track alerts and listen to the authorities. Secondary disaster effects can injure or kill because services we depend on are not available to stop a hazard. If a fire starts in a different neighborhood but the wind carries it into your neighborhood, you are better off evacuating than trying to stay and fight the fire with a few household fire extinguishers or a garden hose. Listen for reports of roads that are open and roads that are closed from the disaster. Update your evacuation plans with this information.

- Take action. If the disaster damaged roads and interrupted the flow of food, water and fuel into a disaster area, can you stay there? This damage, by itself, does not immediately threaten your health and safety. It does make it more dangerous to shelter-in-place. If the authorities are saying that these services, as well as essential services like power and water, will be restored within a few days, then it is worth sheltering-in-place. If the authorities cannot tell you how quickly these services will be restored, or you think you might run out of food and water first, then evacuate.

- Communicate. If you shelter-in-place, talk to local and long-distance contacts. Local contacts can tell you if there are any hazards, like a spreading fire, that might force you to evacuate suddenly. Long-distance contacts can give you updates on what authorities say they are doing and where. In a large disaster area, recovery could take months or longer for very important services to be restored to more remote areas. If you are evacuating, follow the same "communicate" guidance from earlier in this chapter.

IMPORTANT SERVICES & NEEDS

These services and needs are important for long-term health and survival. They include: hospital, postal, school, veterinary, animal control and garbage services.

These are services that meet needs but are not vital to our health or survival here and now. They benefit our long-term health and can help us survive. We would be inconvenienced if many of these services were not available for days to weeks. The loss of these services for months to a year would result in more sickness from disease, untreated or poorly treated injuries and even shorter lives for you, your family or group, and any pets or livestock. The loss of access to schools could set children's learning back a year.

Prepare

- You cannot replace all the services that a hospital performs. You can get first-aid training to help treat injuries. If the roads are still open and you have fuel, you can take a person or most animals to get care that is beyond your skills. You can pay many of your bills using the Internet, and companies like UPS and FedEx may be able to deliver packages, even if it takes longer for you to receive them. Some services, like vaccine delivery in case of an epidemic, will not be available for everyone if there are no postal services. Look at online learning and home-schooling options for your school-age children.

- If you should lose garbage services, you will need to learn about recycling and the benefits of a compost pit. If you plan to burn garbage, keep an extra fire extinguisher nearby. Remember, if disaster effects stop garbage from being picked up, they may also stop fire services from responding if a fire gets out of control. Even if you are careful, you are still in more danger because a neighbor could get careless when burning their garbage.

Protect

- Stay informed. Talk with your local and long-distance contacts so you know what care is available locally. A doctor's office or clinic can help with injuries even if you cannot reach a hospital. Listen to the authorities to know when different services should be restored.

- Take action. Seek help with injuries that you cannot treat. Restock so you have the food, water and medicine you need to take care of yourself and others. Get children into a school routine, whether that is home-schooling in your home or as part of a larger group of people without access to other school options. If public schooling is not available in an area, authorities should be able to offer alternatives to help.

- Recycle paper and plastic, and put yard waste into a compost pit. Control fires used to burn garbage; keep the fire small and stay until it is out. Bring an extra fire extinguisher with you to put the fire out quickly. If it is windy or very dry, do not burn that day. Keep remaining garbage outside the house in sturdy containers. This will reduce attempts by animals to get into the garbage. Get a post office box so that you can receive your mail regularly.

- Communicate. Talk to local and long-distance contacts, check the Internet and follow news updates. Some services will be restored more quickly than others. In a large disaster area, recovery could take months or longer for important services to be restored to more remote areas. You need to decide if the loss of these services is too much for you and your family or group to try to overcome. If you decide to evacuate, follow the same "communicate" guidance from earlier in this chapter.

CONCLUSION

The aftermath of a disaster can leave you without many services that you rely on, and with needs that cannot be met. You know the difference between essential, very important and important services and needs. Your planning and preparation to overcome these losses will help you and others as you work to recover. Take time to reassure children and any who need it. It could take weeks or more to get children used to new routines.

YOUR CHECKLIST —
SECONDARY DISASTER EFFECTS

Prepare For the Loss of Essential, Very Important and Important Services and Needs

❑ Buy a solar-powered charger to recharge devices like cell phones;

❑ Buy a portable water filter;

❑ Buy a generator if you need power to care for a sick family member;

❑ Increase your stock of water and food to seven days or more in your emergency shelter-in-place kit if you don't plan to evacuate regardless of the disaster;

❑ Take first-aid classes so you can perform life-saving first aid and better treat injuries;

❑ Get an extra prescription for any critical medicines you need;

❑ Buy a good pair of walking shoes and break them in before a disaster strikes.

Treat Injuries

❑ Perform life-saving first aid, start breathing, stop bleeding;

❑ Seek emergency medical service aid;

❑ Treat other injuries;

❑ Get an evaluation and treatment of all injuries after the disaster.

ACTIONS AFTER A DISASTER

Examine, Repair Your Shelter After the Disaster Is Over; Decide If You Can Safely Stay

❑ Evacuate if you will have no access to power, water or food for a week or more;

❑ Evacuate if your shelter cannot protect you from weather effects like extreme cold;

Assess What Services Are Still Available In Your Neighborhood and Surrounding Area

❑ If you have enough services and can meet enough of your needs to safely stay for days to weeks, then restock your emergency shelter-in-place kit and work on recovery;

❑ If you do not have enough services or cannot meet enough of your needs to safely stay for the short-term, then evacuate.

Communicate

❑ Tell your local and long-distance contacts your plans;

❑ Listen to updates about where services are available, and restock fuel, water and food;

❑ Share information on the location and types of hazards and services found locally or on your evacuation route.

Notes

Notes

Notes

Chapter 4:
Tornadoes and Hurricanes

SCAN FOR CHAPTER
OVERVIEW VIDEO

Tornadoes and hurricanes are violent types of storms that require planning and preparation to ensure the safety of you and your family or group.

These weather events have extremely high winds that can be devastating to anything in their path. Both are accompanied by severe thunderstorms and possible hail. A hurricane can also be accompanied by flooding and tornado outbreaks. Your planning and preparation will improve your ability to evacuate or safely shelter from these storms.

TORNADOES

WHY SHOULD YOU BE CONCERNED ABOUT TORNADOES?

Tornadoes are intensely violent storms that usually occur in the Midwest, Southwest and Southeast. While occurrences are often associated with a "season" and these regions of the United States, tornadoes can occur in any state at any time of the year.

Modern weather radar technology has vastly improved our ability to understand and identify weather conditions that cause tornadoes. The National Weather Service uses the Watch, Advisory and Warning descriptions discussed in Chapter 2 to tell you what level of danger you face. Even with these tools, however, tornadoes can still occur with little to no warning.

In the U.S., tornadoes usually occur in the months of March through August. From 2008-2010, an average of 1,367 tornadoes occurred, resulting in 192 deaths. In 2011, due to violent tornado outbreaks, deaths from twisters through August reached 549. The increase in deaths in 2011 was the result of a series of large tornado outbreaks, including an EF-5 tornado that hit Joplin, Missouri, causing great loss of life. Tuscaloosa, Alabama, also suffered devastating tornado damage in April 2011.

Many of you have seen the intense images of destruction after a large tornado passes through a populated area. Your preparation before the emergency and your actions when the emergency occurs are key to the safety, and even survival, of you and your family or group.

UNDERSTANDING TORNADOES

What Causes a Tornado?

Tornadoes are caused by warm, humid air in the lower atmosphere, colder air in the upper atmosphere, and the speed at which they rise and fall within the atmosphere. The

turbulence that occurs when these different air currents interact creates conditions that are common in rapidly developing thunderstorms.

Intensity of Tornadoes

Tornadoes are classified using the Enhanced Fujita scale. This scale uses six categories to classify tornadoes based on damage and associated wind speed.

Speed	Wind Scale (mph)	Key Information
EF 0	65–85	• 69 percent of all tornadoes • Less than 1 percent of all tornado deaths
EF 1	86–109	• Light to moderate damage. Example: tree limbs broken, chimneys and roofs of homes damaged, mobile homes moved from foundation
EF 2	110–137	• 29 percent of all tornadoes • 30 percent of all tornado deaths
EF 3	138–167	• Significant to severe damage. Example: Mobile homes destroyed, trees uprooted/snapped, heavy damage to homes, cars overturned
EF 4	168–199	• 2 percent of all tornadoes • 70 percent of all tornado deaths
EF 5	200–234	• Devastating damage. Example: Complete destruction of homes, large buildings damaged, car-size projectiles picked up and hurled hundreds of yards

Tornadoes cause damage, injury and even death. More than two-thirds of all tornadoes cause light to moderate damage and very few deaths. These tornadoes usually last less than 10 minutes. As the wind speed increases, the level of damage and the number of injuries and deaths also increase. Tornadoes rated as EF 2 and EF 3 can have winds from 110 to 167 miles per hour and they usually last less than 20 minutes. The most dangerous tornadoes have wind speeds of more than 167 miles per hour. While only two out of every 100 tornadoes are this dangerous, they cause 70 percent of all tornado-related deaths. They also cause tremendous damage, leveling homes and hurling vehicles hundreds of feet through the air. These tornadoes can last over an hour.

Tornado Hazards

Flying debris is the most significant threat from a tornado. Take shelter away from windows to reduce the chance of injury.

Some people believe that the pressure from a tornado can cause extra damage to a building, so windows should be opened to equalize the pressure, but this is not true. You put yourself and others in danger if you try to open all the windows instead of seeking shelter. You do not want to be near windows when debris and high winds hit them.

Other tornado hazards include hail and lightning. Treat hail like flying debris. If you must shelter away from buildings, do not shelter among trees, thus reducing the chances you will be hit by lightning.

PREPARE BEFORE A TORNADO

Since tornadoes can occur with little or no warning, it is important that your emergency plan includes alternate shelter-in-place locations, like where a member of the family or group works. If family or group members are separated when a tornado strikes, they need to shelter-in-place where they are and look to their own safety. The rest of the family or group can seek shelter together, relying on the emergency shelter-in-place kit. Members who are separated will have to rely on their emergency travel kits to sustain them through the emergency.

Each adult member of the family or group needs to call the local and long-distance contacts, if there is time, to let them know where they are and if they need medical assistance. Contact children who are not with the group and tell them to seek shelter with friends where they are. This is safer than telling children to try to get home when a tornado is coming.

Key Prepare Actions:

- Build your emergency kits and keep them in your home and vehicle(s);
- Store protective coverings near your shelter-in-place location;
- Discuss how your family or group will communicate (cell phone, text and social media). Remember to use ICE (In Case Of Emergency) cell phone numbers;
- Plan to stay informed (portable radio, subscribe to e-mail and text alerts for your area);
- Learn emergency plans for schools, work, daycare and other places you frequent;
- Discuss and practice what you and your family or group will do if a tornado comes. Talk this through with children so that it is not so fearful.

PROTECT DURING A TORNADO

The National Weather Service may announce a Tornado Watch for your area when weather conditions can produce a tornado. In the event of a Tornado Watch, pay attention to sirens, the radio, TV and Internet so you will know if you need to take action. Be prepared to take shelter immediately.

A Tornado Warning means that there is a tornado in your area. Go to your shelter-in-place location now. The list that follows talks about the kind of shelter you should seek, from best to worst. Make sure you bring your emergency shelter-in-place kit with you if it is not in your shelter-in-place location:

- Underground shelter is the best option. Basements and storm cellars will provide the best protection from the effects of high winds and flying debris;
- If you have no underground protection, shelter in an inner room or hallway on the lowest level of the building;
- In a high-rise building, go to an inner hallway or small room on the lowest floor. Stay away from windows, doors and outside walls. Go to the center of the building;
- A trailer, vehicle or mobile home does not provide good protection. Go to a building with a solid foundation. If none is close enough to reach, go to an open area described below;
- If outside in the open, go to a ditch or low-lying area and lie flat.

  Caution: Do not take shelter under a bridge or overpass. This area will act like a wind tunnel and there is a better chance of being hit by debris. You are safer at a flat location.
- Protect your head and eyes from any debris. Parents or other adults need to reassure children and calm their fears. Hold onto any small children and protect their bodies as you are able. Use protective coverings like sleeping bags, heavy coats and thick blankets to help protect from flying debris.
- Stay in the shelter or lie flat outside until the tornado has passed and the flying debris has stopped.

After a Tornado

The effects from a tornado passing through an area can be significant, with damage or even destruction of homes and buildings. Before you leave your shelter, treat any injuries. Treat seriously injured people first, and remember: start breathing, stop bleeding. Call for emergency services to get help treating any serious injuries. Call your long-distance contact and local contact and let them know how you are doing. Call others who had to shelter away from the family or group and direct help to them if they cannot help themselves.

Be careful when you leave your shelter. Make sure that everyone has on good walking shoes to avoid injury from broken glass and other sharp objects. Look at your shelter-in-

place location and the surrounding neighborhood to see whether or not you have the services you need to survive. If you had to shelter away from your home, wait until it is safe to travel then return home. Now, you survived the tornado but can you live in your home? What should you consider?

In Chapter 3, we talked about the essential, very important and important services and needs that we rely on for our long-term health and survival. Use these guidelines to decide whether you can safely live in your home or if you need to evacuate until these services are restored and your needs can be met.

If you need to evacuate, you will rely on your emergency travel kit and any remaining supplies from your shelter-in-place kit to see you out of the disaster area.

HURRICANES
WHY SHOULD YOU BE CONCERNED ABOUT HURRICANES?

Hurricanes are violent, destructive storms that usually form in the Atlantic Ocean. While hurricanes normally threaten the Gulf Coast and East Coast from mid-August to October, they can occur at any time of the year.

Hurricanes can be devastating when they hit land. High winds, storm surge and flooding cause most of the damage. Since 2000, there have been over 16 hurricanes in the United States resulting in more than an estimated 1,600 deaths and $150 billion of damage.

UNDERSTANDING HURRICANES
What Causes a Hurricane?

Hurricanes are caused by warm water that creates a tropical disturbance and provides energy to a storm. These disturbances occur when the water temperature in the ocean is 80 degrees or higher. Warm, humid air continually rises, cools and drops, creating a cyclone with high winds and rain.

When winds from the storm become greater than 39 mph, the storm is considered a "Tropical Storm" and given a name. If the winds of the storm become greater than a sustained 74 mph, it is considered a hurricane and given a category rating.

In a normal year, 11 tropical storms will form over the Atlantic Ocean, Caribbean Sea and Gulf of Mexico. An average of six of these will become hurricanes each year. Over a three-year period, an average of five hurricanes will make landfall in the United States. As a hurricane or tropical storm hits land, it is no longer fueled by high water temperatures and begins to lose energy. It is common for a hurricane to be "downgraded" to a tropical storm after landfall. (Note: A typhoon or cyclone is the term used for storms of hurricane strength in the western Pacific Ocean. These storms usually do not reach the continental U.S., but sometimes remnants of eastern Pacific Ocean typhoons make landfall in the southwestern states).

Intensity of Hurricanes

Hurricanes are rated using the Saffir-Simpson scale. This scale, based on wind speed, is used to categorize the intensity of the hurricane.

Hurricane damage increases with rising wind speeds, much like tornado damage. However, in the case of a hurricane, the wind also causes storm surges that lead to flooding, additional damage and other hazards. For example, Hurricane Katrina created a major storm surge that contributed to the flooding of the New Orleans area. Katrina, a Category 5 hurricane, caused an estimated 1,500 deaths and $125 billion of damage.

Category	Wind Speed (mph)	Storm Surge (ft)	Key Information
1**	74–95	4–5	• 81 percent of all U.S. hurricanes* • Minimum to moderate damage • Structural damage to mobile homes and poorly constructed wood frame homes, including collapse
2	96–110	6–8	• Windows broken • Tree limbs snapped • Shoreline flooding • Commercial signage damaged • Electricity lost
3	111–130	9–12	• 13 percent of all U.S. hurricanes* • Extensive to extreme damage • Mobile homes and poorly constructed wood frame homes could be destroyed • Well-constructed homes badly damaged
4	131–155	13–18	• Majority of windows broken • High percentage of gabled roofs torn free • Trees uprooted and snapped • Inland flooding • Electricity lost for an extended period
5	>155	>18	• 6 percent of all U.S. hurricanes* • Catastrophic damage • Complete collapse of mobile homes and poorly constructed wood frame homes • High percentage of low-rise and commercial buildings destroyed • Major damage to high-rise and well-constructed buildings • Large trees uprooted and snapped • Significant inland flooding • Electricity lost for extended period

*2000–2010 data ** Similar damage expected from a tropical storm*

Hurricane Hazards

Flying debris, structural damage and flooding are the most significant threats from a hurricane. If you live on a coast, plan for a hurricane even if there is only a small chance one will occur. If you live in an evacuation area, learn the evacuation routes and monitor evacuation orders. You may not have to evacuate for every hurricane, but planning gives you a better chance to evacuate safely if you need to.

Evacuation from the area, or moving to a strong evacuation shelter, will improve the safety of you and others. Only shelter-in-place if you believe that your shelter is more than strong enough to protect you from the primary disaster effects of the coming storm. Remember that you may rely on services that are not as well protected as you are. Do you believe that the storm will cause significant structural damage that will prevent you from receiving power, water, food and other services for weeks? If you do, then evacuation may still be the best answer.

PREPARE

Hurricanes come with warnings that are widely broadcast by media and government. You should know if a hurricane is coming, how strong it will be and whether there is an evacuation order well before it reaches land.

Take action to improve the safety of you and others, and potentially reduce the damage to your home and property. These are the terms you should understand as you follow news about the approaching storm:

- Tropical Storm Watch: This is an announcement that tropical storm conditions are *possible* in a specified coastal area within 48 hours;
- Tropical Storm Warning: This is an announcement that tropical storm conditions are *expected* in a specified coastal area within 36 hours;
- Hurricane Watch: This is an announcement that hurricane conditions are *possible* within a specified coastal area. Because of the need to prepare, a hurricane warning is issued 48 hours in advance of the anticipated arrival of tropical storm force winds;
- Hurricane Warning: This is an announcement that hurricane conditions are *expected* somewhere in a specified coastal region. Because of the need to prepare, a hurricane watch is issued 36 hours in advance of the anticipated arrival of tropical storm-force winds.

Local governments make the decision to issue evacuation orders. These decisions are made based on considerations such as: the expected size and path of the storm; the expected size and location of any storm surge; how many people will be affected; and how long it will take to notify, organize and evacuate those in danger.

Key Prepare Actions:

- Build your emergency kits and store supplies needed to protect your home and shelter-in-place location. Keep the kits in your home and vehicle(s);
- Clear dead wood, trim trees and shrubs in your yard to reduce storm debris when the high winds come;
- Store protective coverings, like sleeping bags and thick blankets, near your shelter-in-place location;
- Discuss where you and your family or group will meet and how you will communicate (cell phone, text and social media). Remember to use ICE (In Case Of Emergency) cell phone numbers;
- Plan to stay informed (portable radio, subscribe to e-mail and text alerts for your area);
- Create a notebook that shows evacuation routes and pre-approved evacuation centers in your area;
- Learn the routes and actual location of the centers before the start of the hurricane season;
- Coordinate with family and friends outside the likely disaster area for a place to stay if you need to evacuate;
- Discuss and practice what you and your family or group will do if a hurricane comes. If you have children, you can even take a trip to an evacuation center and along part of the evacuation route. Discuss why you are doing this and encourage questions to increase their comfort with staying in an evacuation center or evacuating away from a hurricane.

PROTECT PRIOR TO LANDFALL

You know a hurricane is coming, so it is time to act. Review the status of evacuation routes and evacuation centers as you monitor the approaching storm. Remember, it is better to evacuate before an evacuation order is given. When you evacuate after the order is given, you can only evacuate at the speed of the crowd.

Key Protect Actions:

- Fill your car with gasoline early in the alert stage;
- Cover all of your home's windows with pre-cut plywood or hurricane shutters;
- Bring in any outdoor pets;
- Bring in all yard furniture, decorations and anything else that might become projectiles in high winds;
- Secure your home and evacuate or shelter-in-place.

If you are not able to evacuate, stay indoors and away from all windows. Take shelter in an inner room with no windows. Stay in your shelter until local authorities say it is safe to leave.

If you evacuate, take and provide for your pets. Remember that many evacuation centers only allow for service animals, so plan accordingly.

PROTECT DURING LANDFALL

During the storm, local authorities and contacts may not be able to provide immediate information on the storm, because they are sheltering, too. Listen to your weather radio, check the TV and Internet, and talk to your long-distance contacts so you are aware of storm changes that could affect you. Remain in the evacuation center or shelter until the storm passes. Do not emerge from shelter until confirmation by authorities that it is safe.

After a Hurricane

Once a hurricane passes, you will have to overcome secondary disaster effects. Flooding, downed power lines, and structural damage to buildings and roads are all potential hazards to be careful of. You should:

- Watch out for flooding. If floodwaters are rising or a flash flood warning is issued, seek high ground;
- Stay out of floodwaters. The water may be contaminated, contain an electrical charge, or be dangerously fast. If you are in your vehicle and trapped by rising water, get out and move to high ground immediately;
- Tornadoes often occur during hurricanes. Be alert and take shelter in the event of a tornado;
- Stay away from downed power lines and surrounding water;
- Do not return to your home until local authorities say it is safe. Even after the water has receded, there may be damage to roads and buildings;
- Drink only bottled or purified water until authorities confirm the safety of the local water supply.

You should have food, water and supplies for at least three days in your emergency kit.

YOUR CHECKLIST — TORNADOES AND HURRICANES

Prepare For Primary Disaster Effects — Tornadoes

❑ Store protective coverings near your shelter-in-place location;

❑ Discuss how your family or group will communicate (cell phone, text and social media). Remember to use ICE (In Case Of Emergency) cell phone numbers;

❑ Plan to stay informed (portable radio, subscribe to e-mail and text alerts for your area);

❑ Learn emergency plans for schools, work, daycare and other places you frequent;

❑ Discuss and practice what you and your family or group will do if a tornado comes. Talk through this with children so that it is not so fearful.

Protect From Primary Disaster Effects — Tornadoes

❑ Seek shelter now;

❑ Choose your best option: Shelter underground, or shelter in an inner room or hallway on the lowest level of a building. If possible, shelter in a building with a solid foundation;

❑ Stay away from windows, doors and outside walls. Go to the center of the building;

❑ If outside in the open, go to a ditch or low-lying area and lie flat;

❑ *Do not shelter in a trailer, vehicle or mobile home;* it is better to shelter outside.

Prepare For Primary Disaster Effects — Hurricanes

❑ Keep supplies needed to board up windows;

❑ Create a book with community evacuation centers and evacuation routes;

❑ Rehearse evacuation routes;

❑ Identify and discuss where your family or group will meet;

❑ Learn all emergency and shelter-in-place plans for schools, daycare facilities and work locations.

Protect From Primary Disaster Effects — Hurricanes

❑ Fill your car with gasoline early in the alert stage;

❑ Cover all of your home's windows with pre-cut plywood or hurricane shutters;

❑ Bring in any outdoor pets;

❑ Bring in all yard furniture, decorations and anything else that might become projectiles in high winds;

❑ Secure your home, and evacuate or shelter-in-place;

❑ Check radio, TV and Internet, and talk to your long-distance contacts so you know about storm changes that could affect you.

For actions after the disaster, see page 57.

Notes

Notes

Notes

Chapter 5:
Extreme Winter Storms, Blizzards & Ice

Scan For Chapter Overview Video

Extreme winter storms, blizzards and ice events occur when the temperature is near or below freezing. These storms can include a combination of ice, snow, drifting snow and extreme cold.

You may not expect to see some of these winter effects if you live in the Deep South or on the West Coast, but this is no guarantee that you will not have to overcome some or all of these effects. It is simply less likely you will face a winter storm that causes them.

Your planning and preparation will help you overcome these effects while reducing the chance of injury, or worse.

WHY SHOULD YOU BE CONCERNED?

These storms are more common in the central and northern part of the United States, but some of the worst storms we have seen recently brought winter storm effects as far south as the border with Mexico. In early 2011, a winter storm called the Groundhog Day Blizzard struck. It brought freezing temperatures and drifting snow from Ciudad Juarez in Mexico, across New Mexico, Texas and the Midwest, and up into Canada. This storm blanketed some areas with one to two feet of snow, while others saw ice accumulations of more than an inch. There were even tornadoes reported at the front edge of the storm as it advanced north. The storm may have affected almost 100 million people, with the related ice storm causing $1 billion in damage by itself.

WHAT CAUSES EXTREME COLD-RELATED WEATHER?

The air currents that can cause tornadoes can also help cause these storms if the conditions are right. These storms can occur when temperatures are near or below freezing and two large air masses collide. One air mass is typically very cold air while the other is warm air and carries a significant amount of moisture. The result can be a mix of snow, drifting snow, ice and other effects. These results are determined by a number of factors, including the size of the storm and its accompanying winds, how much moisture the storm is carrying, and the temperature of the ground it passes over. You cannot guarantee you will be missed by the storm, on the edge of it, or in the center of the storm. But you can prepare and protect from the effects of the storm and its aftermath.

DISASTER EFFECTS & HAZARDS

You will have to prepare for and protect from high winds, extreme cold, snow, drifting snow, sleet, freezing rain and ice. There are hazards that come with these effects and they can injure or kill just as readily. They include frostbite, hypothermia and overexertion, from shoveling snow for example. During and after the storm, you may have to overcome drifting snow, slippery roads and walkways, bitter cold and even power outages.

The National Weather Service will issue Watches and Warnings for these storms. Remember, a "Watch" means the conditions are possible for the named storm while a "Warning" means the named storm is occurring or will occur soon.

Your greatest dangers from these types of storms are extreme cold, possible loss of power, and slippery roads and walkways. Add in the potential for limited visibility due to heavy snow or blizzard conditions, and the danger increases. You are most vulnerable if you are outside when one of these storms strike.

If you are not at your shelter-in-place location when the Winter Storm Warning occurs, return to it or seek shelter elsewhere. The greatest danger during this storm is to be caught away from shelter and its security. Your vehicle can shelter you from the effects of the storm for a few hours, but it is not where you want to shelter for a day or more.

PREPARE BEFORE THE STORM

While these storms usually come with some advance warning, you do not want to wait for a Winter Storm Watch to be declared before getting ready for severe winter weather.

Plan to stay informed. If you have warning of a coming storm and can work from home, do so. If anyone is in school, check with the school so you understand their policy regarding very bad weather. Discuss who will pick up a child if the school closes early. You can adjust your schedule when a "snow day" is declared before the start of the school day. It can be more difficult for one of two working parents to pick up a child from school or meet them at the house when school closes unexpectedly in the middle of the day. Now, focus your preparations on your vehicle and your shelter-in-place location.

Maintain your vehicle by following the guidance provided in Chapter 2. In addition, consider carrying several bags of cat litter or sand in the back or trunk of your vehicle. This will give you added weight for traction in slippery conditions and can be poured over ice to help you get past a slippery patch of roadway. If required for safety, make sure you have four good snow tires or chains for areas where you live and plan to travel through during the winter months. Keep a good windshield scraper in your vehicle and make sure your windshield washer fluid is full.

Update your emergency travel kit. Replace summer seasonal clothing and supplies with your winter needs. This includes gloves, hats, winter boots and blankets. Refill your kit with water bottles, snack food and high-calorie food bars. If you are planning on a long trip and may encounter extreme winter weather, pack extra water and food just in case you are forced to seek shelter in your car or at a location with limited or no food and water, like a rest area.

Maintain your shelter-in-place location by following the guidance provided in Chapter 2. In addition, take steps to weatherize your home and any locations where you and your family or group will shelter-in-place. Weatherization should include at least the following: caulk windows; weatherstrip outside doors, including doors to a porch or garage; and, if you have an attic, make sure your insulation covers the attic access door. This will help reduce the loss of heat, reduce your power bill and improve your ability to stay — even if you lose power. If you have the ability to safely heat your shelter-in-place location with an alternate fuel, like wood or coal, store extra fuel for heating. Make sure all smoke will be properly vented away from your shelter location.

Update your emergency shelter-in-place kit. Add extra blankets, clothing, hat, scarf, coat, pair of gloves or mittens and winter boots for each person who will use your shelter location. This becomes even more important for those who will shelter away from their homes. Store at least one snow shovel near or in your shelter location. You can also add additional water containers like plastic two-liter soda bottles or five-gallon water storage containers. You can store water for extra days to weeks using these containers. Avoid using old milk containers; the milk residue is difficult to clean out, making it easier for bacteria to grow.

PROTECT FROM THE STORM

A Winter Storm Watch has been declared, so there is a good chance you will be affected by the storm. You know your area and the kind of roads you will travel on to get important supplies, like prescription medications, before you go home. If you need supplies and you did not get stocked up before the Watch was declared, get them now. Give yourself extra time to buy groceries and winter supplies that have run short from prior use. Make sure your vehicle has a full tank of gas. You are now competing with the crowd for items that could be in short supply.

Stay Informed

Follow news of the storm. If you are traveling, call a contact at your destination, check the Internet and make sure it is still safe to continue your journey. You may be driving out of the predicted path of the storm. If you are not, reconsider your travel. If it is an emergency, then travel unless the authorities have closed roads you would use or declared a travel emergency for part of your travel path. If you are traveling by air, check with your airline or the airport you are flying from and make sure your flight has not been delayed or canceled.

If you must travel, take extra care to ensure your vehicle is ready for the journey and conditions. Ensure that your emergency travel kit is fully stocked, and let contacts know about your trip, when you leave, the route you are taking and when you expect to arrive at your destination. Dress warmly in layers and consider putting your emergency travel kit inside the vehicle instead of in the trunk. You want to be able to reach the kit without having to leave the vehicle to open the trunk. If possible, do not travel alone in these conditions. Two people have a chance to get a vehicle out of a snow bank where one person would find it difficult.

If you have children, watch for an alert from any schools or daycare centers so you know when they will need to be picked up or when bus services will be dropping them off. If an adult is near the school(s) and they are authorized to pick up the children, consider doing this. You and the children will avoid what could be hours spent on a bus waiting for them to reach your neighborhood while the weather just gets worse. Contact any school-age children who are driving and make sure they know to drive home as soon as they are released from school.

Be prepared for the Winter Storm Watch to become a Winter Storm Warning. Remember that some effects, like freezing rain and ice accumulation, can occur before the snow and bitter cold reach you.

Take Action

The extreme winter storm is coming or it is already here. Did everyone get to your shelter-in-place location? Are all school-age children home? Call your local contact and ask about anyone in your family or group that has not reached your shelter location or called you. Anyone separated from your group should seek shelter elsewhere if they cannot safely return to your location. They do not want to be stranded on the road and risk having to wait out the storm from inside their vehicle.

Your preparations before the storm are paying off. You are at your shelter location and you have food, water and any needed medicine. If you have power and heat, you can just wait out the storm. If you lose power or you have limited fuel for heating your home, like wood or coal for example, consider closing vents and doors in rooms that will not be used. This will reduce the loss of heat and help you conserve your fuel. If you have a wood-burning fireplace, be sure to close the damper once the fire is completely out. Remember: do not run an emergency generator inside your home or shelter-in-place location, because the exhaust includes carbon monoxide, which can kill you.

If there is a warning that you could lose water pressure, consider filling a bathtub and extra containers with water. Use this extra water for personal hygiene. It can also be used to fill the toilet tank so you can flush, and continue to go to the bathroom inside.

If you lose water pressure before you can do this, gather snow in buckets and dump it in the bathtub. Do not use snowmelt for drinking or personal hygiene unless you purify the water first.

A large snowstorm with drifting snow could bury your driveway, while an ice storm could turn it into an ice-skating rink. Follow the weather forecast and decide what you need to do. You may need to go out and shovel the driveway several times throughout the storm so that clearing the driveway is a manageable task. If you do, dress warmly and be careful not to overexert yourself shoveling snow. Frostbite from the cold and a heart attack from overexertion are both hazards that are less likely to occur when you limit your exposure to the cold and take periodic breaks from shoveling snow. When there is ice and you must walk or drive on it, carefully put salt or sand down ahead of where you walk so you are less likely to slip. If you are going to try to remove the ice by hand, consider putting down salt first then using an ice chopper once the ice has started to melt.

Sometimes, a storm can catch you away from your shelter. If you are driving, stay on well-traveled highways and avoid back roads. Let your local contact know where you are, who is with you and where you are going. Try to get to your shelter-in-place location. If you cannot safely reach this location, find another location to shelter in and wait out the storm. Call your local contact and let them know where you are sheltering.

If the storm has trapped you in your vehicle, pull all the way off the highway so you will not be hit by a snowplow or another vehicle. Put on your hazard lights and call your local and long-distance contacts to let them know your situation and where you are. They can contact the authorities to get you help and give you updates on attempts to reach you. Get the extra clothing and blankets from your emergency travel kit. Use the clothing as insulation or add layers if you are not dressed warmly enough. Get under the blankets and huddle with anyone you are traveling with to stay warm.

You should only run the vehicle and heater for 10 to 15 minutes an hour. Check the tailpipe and make sure it is clear before starting the vehicle. Also open your window slightly for ventilation and to make sure the tailpipe stays clear while the vehicle is running. At night, turn on the light in your vehicle while it is running so that potential rescuers can better find you. Limit your use of the heater and light when the vehicle is off or you will run down the battery. Turn your hazard lights off once you are no longer a danger to traffic or they will also run down your battery. If you are not alone, take turns sleeping so that there is always someone awake to flag down rescuers.

Do not leave your vehicle unless you see a better shelter in easy walking distance, or if your vehicle has no power or gas and can no longer shelter you. You do not know how deep the snow is and it is often easier for rescuers to find you if you stay in or near your car. If you leave your vehicle, be prepared to carry your emergency travel kit with you so you have food, water and supplies when you need them.

Communicate

When the storm has passed, you may face drifting snow, ice, downed power lines and other obstacles. Treat injuries and seek help for those that are beyond your skills. Road conditions may cause a slow response from emergency medical services, so early notification is critical if someone faces a life-threatening injury.

Check your shelter-in-place location and supplies. If your shelter is not damaged and you still have power, water and food, you should be able to stay while services are restored and roads are cleared. If your shelter is no longer safe to stay in or it is too cold to safely stay, talk to your contacts and the authorities to try to find a new place to stay until your shelter can be repaired. Whether you can stay or must leave your shelter location, call your contacts and let them know how you are doing.

If you had to seek shelter away from your chosen shelter-in-place location, call your local and long-distance contacts. Tell them your status and call for the authorities if you cannot reach your vehicle or it is snowbound. Try to stay warm until help arrives.

YOUR CHECKLIST — EXTREME WINTER STORMS, BLIZZARDS & ICE

Prepare For Primary Disaster Effects — Extreme Winter Storms, Blizzards & Ice

❑ Put several bags of cat litter or sand in the back or trunk of your vehicle;

❑ Store a good windshield scraper in your vehicle and make sure your windshield washer fluid is full;

❑ Update your emergency travel kit by replacing summer seasonal clothing and supplies with your winter needs, including gloves, hats, winter boots and blankets;

❑ Weatherize your home and any locations where you and your family or group will shelter-in-place;

❑ Store extra fuel for heating your shelter and your food;

❑ Update your emergency shelter-in-place kit by adding extra blankets, clothing, and an extra hat, scarf, coat, pair of gloves or mittens and winter boots for each person who will use your shelter location;

❑ Put at least one snow shovel near your shelter location;

❑ Store additional containers, like plastic two-liter soda bottles or five-gallon water cans for water storage, near your shelter location.

Protect From Primary Disaster Effects — Extreme Winter Storms, Blizzards & Ice

❑ Fill your vehicle with gas before the storm hits;

❑ Dress warmly and in layers;

❑ Follow alerts, and make sure children at schools and daycare centers are picked up;

❑ *If you reached your shelter,* call your local and long-distance contacts to let them know your situation, who is with you and where you are;

    ❑ If you lose heat, close vents and doors in rooms that will not be used;

    ❑ Close the dampers to wood-burning fireplaces once fires are completely out;

    ❑ Fill a bathtub and extra containers with water;

    ❑ Take turns digging out from drifting snow to avoid overexertion and frostbite;

    ❑ Do not run an emergency generator in your home or shelter-in-place location to avoid breathing carbon monoxide;

❑ *If you are on the road,* check to ensure you are not traveling into the storm;

    ❑ Let contacts know about your trip, when you leave, the route you are taking and when you expect to arrive at your destination;

    ❑ Stay on well-traveled highways and avoid back roads;

    ❑ Seek shelter elsewhere if you cannot safely return to your shelter-in-place location.

❑ *If the storm has trapped you in your vehicle,* pull all the way off the highway;

- ❏ Call your local and long-distance contacts to let them know your situation and where you are;
- ❏ Huddle with other passengers, and use extra clothing and blankets to stay warm;
- ❏ Only run the vehicle and heater for 10 to 15 minutes an hour;
- ❏ At night, turn on your inside vehicle light so potential rescuers can better find you;
- ❏ Take turns sleeping so there is always someone awake to flag down rescuers;
- ❏ Stay with your vehicle unless you have to leave for safety; wait for rescue.

For actions after the disaster, see page 57.

Notes

Notes

Notes

Chapter 6:
Heavy Precipitation & Flooding

SCAN FOR CHAPTER
OVERVIEW VIDEO

Water is often considered the most powerful and potentially destructive natural force on Earth. Anyone who has stood overlooking the Grand Canyon has most likely marveled that a relatively small flow like the Colorado River carved one of the most impressive natural landmarks in the United States. The canyon is 277 miles long, spans 18 miles at its widest point and is over a mile deep. It took millions of years of erosion for water to carve this canyon. The canyon walls bear the signs of many floods over the years.

Flooding is one of the disasters you face wherever you live. It can cause injury, death and destruction on a great scale. During the 20th century, floods were the No. 1 natural disaster in terms of lives lost and property damage.

WHY SHOULD YOU BE CONCERNED?

Heavy precipitation and flooding can occur at anytime of the year, day or night. Most deaths occur when people are swept away by flood currents. These flood waters can also cause significant property damage, with the ability to erode the foundations of buildings and bridges, if they are not destroyed outright.

The Great Mississippi and Missouri River Flood of 1993, also known as the Great Flood of 1993, was caused by long periods of heavy rain from May through September and resulted in many rivers overflowing their banks. It is considered one of the most destructive floods in U.S. history and affected a nine-state region including Illinois, Iowa, Kansas, Minnesota, Missouri, Nebraska, North Dakota, South Dakota and Wisconsin. It caused the deaths of an estimated 48 people and destroyed more than 1,000 levees, as well as 50,000 homes, bridges and buildings. The flooding spread to cover 400,000 square miles and took over seven months to fully recede. Damages exceeded $15 billion.

Flash floods can be extremely dangerous because they are harder to predict and they can occur with little to no warning. A 1972 flash flood in Rapid City, South Dakota, was caused by a slow-moving thunderstorm that brought 15 inches of rain over a five-hour period. That flood killed 237 people.

Floods and flash floods can be treacherous — they can put you and your family or group in immediate danger. Your preparation and planning can help you and others avoid injury or worse, and help you protect your property from flooding.

WHAT CAUSES FLOODING?

Flooding is often caused by periods of heavy precipitation that happen very quickly, or over a longer period of time, what could be weeks to months. This heavy precipitation does not have to occur in the area that is flooded. It can occur upstream, leading to flooding as water moves downstream. During some unusually wet winters, snowstorms cause a great deal of snow to accumulate during the winter months. Once spring comes, the snow melts, creating floods as the rivers carry the snowmelt downstream to lakes or oceans. Flooding can also be caused when man-made structures — like dams or levees — break down, creating a new path for the water to move into. Some specific kinds of floods are listed below:

Flash floods occur very quickly and are often caused by violent or slow-moving storms. They can happen with little or no warning and are particularly dangerous because of the rapid rise of water and the speed of the flood currents. Flash floods can happen in seconds or over several hours. They can occur more easily if the soil is saturated so it cannot absorb any more water, or if storm-drain systems in cities or towns overflow so water has no place to go but into low-lying roads and underpasses. In areas with hills or mountains, steep slopes will also channel water along ravines and low-lying areas, making roads and bridges in those areas more dangerous.

Regional floods can often occur seasonally when the ground is saturated due to long periods of rainfall. Spring rains and melting snow can cause rivers to overflow their banks. These floods are often caused by heavy precipitation from slow-moving storms, hurricanes and tropical storms.

Levee- and dam-break floods are caused when water pressure, water levels or other factors cause these structures to fail. When a break occurs, you may not have much warning to evacuate. If you are near the levee or dam when it breaks, you may have to protect from the effects of a flash flood.

Storm-surge floods are caused by intense storms with winds that push rising water onto otherwise dry land. These floods are usually associated with coastal regions and very intense storms like tropical storms or hurricanes. The effect of wind, waves and rising waters can create strong, dangerous currents.

Ice-jam floods occur on rivers that are totally or partially frozen. The rising water can break up the ice and cause it to build up in shallow areas or jam on obstructions like bridges and logs. The ice jam creates a temporary dam that causes the water level behind the dam to rise and overflow the banks of the river. When the ice jam breaks, the flooding moves downstream and can create flash floods.

Mudflows, debris and landslides are created from the buildup of soil, rocks, fallen trees and other debris in a channel to form a temporary dam. Much like ice-jam floods, the water behind the dam quickly rises, overflowing the top of the channel, resulting in flooding. When the dam fails, water rushes downstream, often generating flash floods.

DISASTER EFFECTS & HAZARDS

You will have to prepare for and protect from effects including fast-moving water, dangerous currents and debris carried by water, ranging from rocks to trees, vehicles and even houses. Low air and water temperatures associated with ice-jam and cold-weather floods make hypothermia — a dangerous heat loss from the cold — another disaster effect you should prepare for. The most dangerous type of flooding is a flash flood. This can be caused by short, intense periods of rainfall, as well as dam or levee breaks. Most flood-related deaths are caused by flash floods. Over 50 percent of all flash-flood deaths are from people getting caught in a flash flood while in their vehicles.

Rising, rapidly moving water is the most dangerous hazard in any flood. People and animals can be swept away and drowned. Houses can be moved off their foundations and even carried downstream. Six inches of water can cause passenger vehicles to lose control and stall. A foot of water can float most passenger vehicles. Two feet of rushing floodwater can cause cars, trucks and utility vehicles to be swept away.

Floodwater can pose a significant danger to your shelter-in-place location and your home. Your walls and furniture will act like a sponge and soak up the floodwater. When it recedes, it will leave behind sediment, debris and even sewage. Vehicles caught in a flood can suffer major electrical damage or worse. Flooding can also cause significant amounts of erosion, damaging the foundations of bridges and buildings, and even causing them to collapse and be swept away. The combination of forest fires followed by heavy precipitation and flooding can also lead to landslides and mudslides in hills and mountains.

Flooding can disrupt or stop many of the essential, very important and important services you rely on. You could face boil advisories because the local water-treatment plant was flooded. Gas and electrical services could be disrupted, possibly for an extended time. Road, rail and transportation services could be shut down due to damage or destruction of highways and bridges.

PREPARE BEFORE FLOODING

In Chapter 2 you learned about the primary disaster effects associated with water. Your chief danger is the risk flooding will impact you and your family or group, or reach your home and/or shelter location. Do you live in a flood plain or in an area where flash floods occurred in the past, like the desert or a hilly or mountainous area? Do you live on relatively high ground that rarely floods or have you had problems with flooding before? Is your children's daycare or school safe from rapidly rising floodwaters?

Meet with your family or group and choose a shelter-in-place location that is safe from flooding. If you live on a flood plain, check with the authorities and your local contacts to identify a shelter location that is safer than your home. Contact your children's daycare or school and ask what they will do to protect your children in the event a flood occurs and there is no time to reach one or more children. Discuss this with your school-age children

and help them understand how important it is to follow the teacher's instructions and get to higher ground or an upper floor in the school building. Sign up for any alert service the school has. For those with pets, choose a location that will allow you to keep them with you. Public shelters will have restrictions about pets that are not service animals helping those with some form of disability.

Maintain your vehicle by following the guidance provided in Chapter 2. Keep your emergency travel kit fully stocked, including several thick, waterproof zip-lock bags, and add an extra blanket and seasonal clothing for each person evacuating with you. Identify multiple evacuation routes and try to avoid low-lying bridges and roads since they are more likely to be closed due to flood effects. Plan to make the evacuation decision with enough time to get away from rising floodwaters. Do not wait until the last minute to evacuate.

If you live in a flood plain or low-lying area, prepare your home each fall for possible flooding. Your goal is to prevent water from entering your home. Identify and fix potential drainage issues around your home such as window wells and slopes that direct water toward the home. This can help avoid getting water into your first floor or basement during or following periods of heavy precipitation. Make sure your sump pump is in good working order. Think about getting a battery backup so it will continue to work even if you

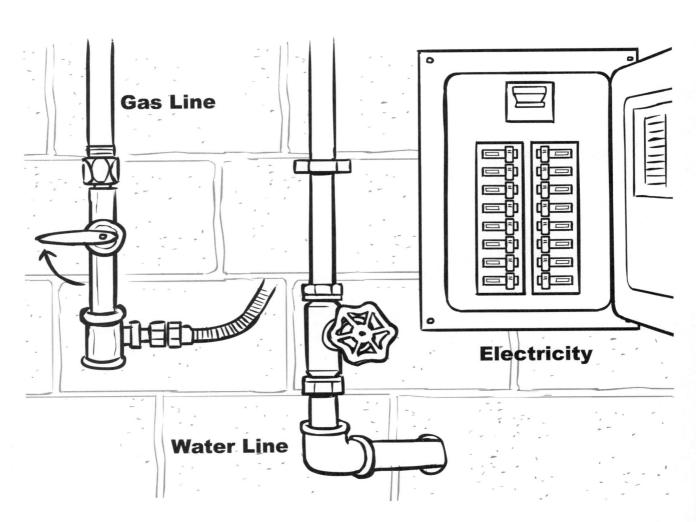

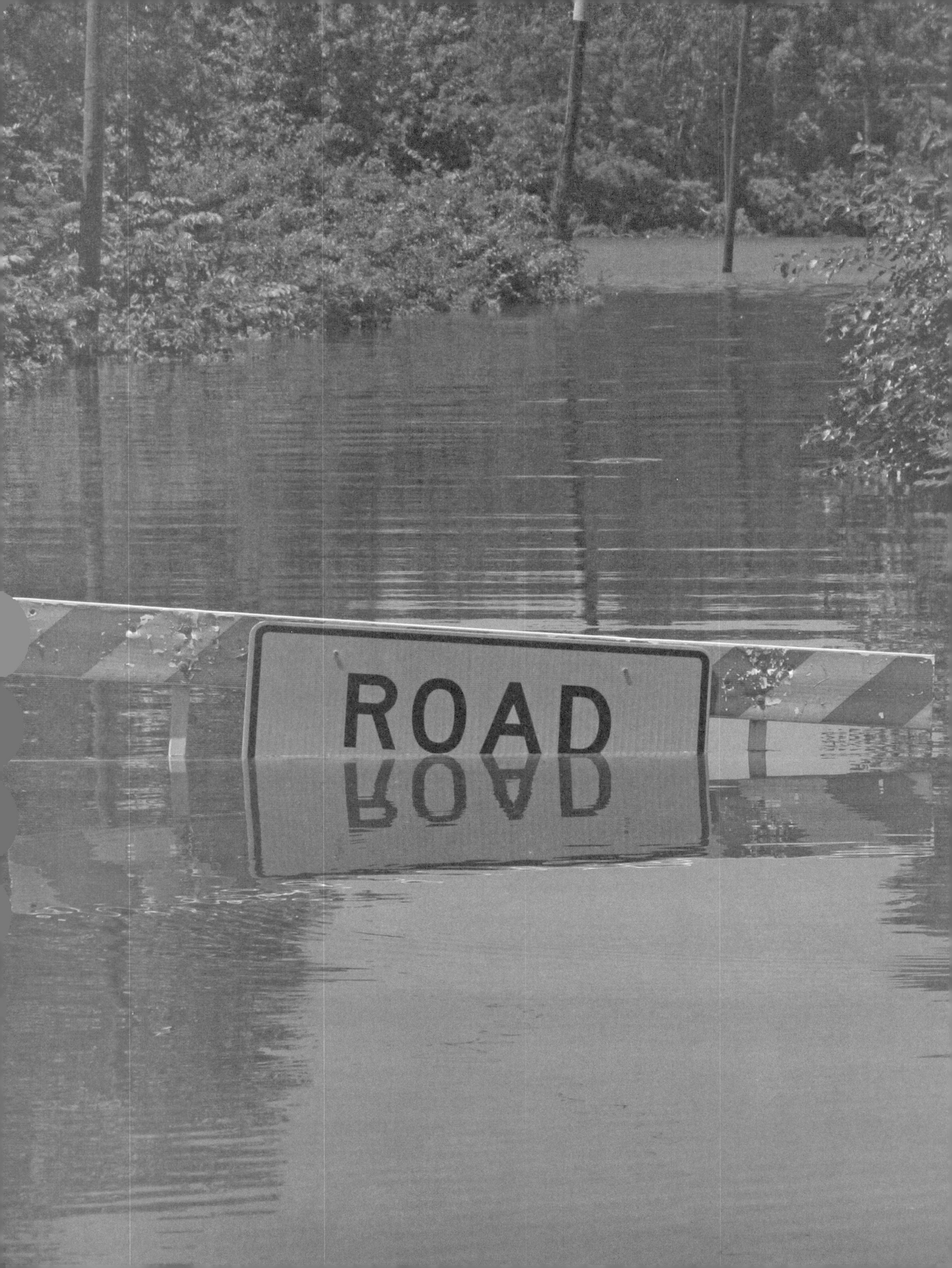
ROAD

lose power for a period of time. Consider using sandbags or other materials to create a short wall around your home to stop small floods, but it likely will not stop water three or more feet deep rushing swiftly through your neighborhood.

Prepare the inside of your home for easier clean-up and recovery from a flood. Move sensitive items and valuables out of the lower level as time permits. Anything in the lowest level could be destroyed with as little as six inches of standing water in your home. For more information on how to prepare your home for flooding, go to the following website: http://www.fema.gov/library/viewRecord.do?id=1420.

Stock your shelter-in-place kit and store it up high enough where it is unlikely a flood could damage it. Use waterproof bags and containers to protect food, medicine, clothing and electronics. If you are forced to evacuate and you have time and space, take this kit with you.

Protect From Flooding

There is a Flash Flood Watch for your area or you hear an announcement that a local river will soon exceed flood stage, and flooding could spread to where you live. What do you do?

Stay Informed

Follow the news regarding flood alerts for your area. Flash floods can be deadly, and local news stations will broadcast flash flood alerts for areas at risk. The National Weather Service will issue Watches, Advisories and Warnings for floods and flash floods. Remember that these go from the least dangerous, a Watch, to the most dangerous, a Warning. These alerts may give you time to evacuate to safety.

When traveling during a storm, particularly through mountainous or desert regions, tune your radio to local weather or news to listen for potential warnings. Flash floods can easily wash vehicles from roads and create very deadly situations. Ensure that your long-distance contacts know about your trip, when you are leaving and when you expect to reach your destination. Let them know about any changes the storm may force in your travel plans or route and when you arrive.

Be prepared for the Watch to become a Warning. If you know you are at risk because you live in a flood plain or are in the path a seasonal flash flood often takes, evacuate before the Warning is issued. If you evacuate once the Warning is issued, you could be in your vehicle trying to leave when the floodwaters reach you.

Take Action

A Flood Warning has been declared for your area. You have done what you can to prepare and protect your home from floodwaters. If you have time and you need to evacuate, you should shut off your gas, water and electricity at the main switches or valves, unplug electrical appliances, and then move valuables to shelving or an upper floor. Do not try to unplug electrical appliances if you are wet or standing in water. Evacuate the area, if possible, or at least get to higher ground, like your second floor or roof if you have no better options. If you don't need to evacuate, you and your family or group should shelter-in-place and wait for the flood emergency to end.

Anyone separated from the family or group must evacuate or shelter-in-place as best they can. Call your long-distance contacts and let them know your status and who is with you. If you are on the road when a Flash Flood Warning is declared, get to higher ground! Avoid roads and bridges in low-lying areas and valleys, and do not try to cross running water. If your vehicle is caught in running water, leave it behind and get to higher ground if you can do this safely. Be careful leaving your vehicle and getting through the water. Even six inches of quickly moving water can knock you off your feet.

You chose your shelter-in-place location because it should be safe from a flood or flash flood. Once you reach this location, focus on taking care of your family or group. Periodically check your shelter and make sure it is not in danger from the flooding. If the flood becomes much worse than predicted, and it threatens your shelter location, you could be forced to evacuate. The extended loss of essential services — like those that provide power, water and food — could also force you to evacuate. If you need evacuation assistance, call your long-distance contacts and the local authorities to get help.

Communicate

Once the flood is over, listen to the news and check the Internet. Call your long-distance contacts to help coordinate reuniting anyone separated from the family or group, and help everyone gather back together.

If you had to evacuate, can you return home? Check with the authorities and any local contacts that may have stayed. Are services you depend on — like water, power and access to food — available in your area? If they are and the authorities are allowing people to return to their homes, then you should be able to return home. Have your utilities checked and turned back on by professionals. Restock your shelter-in-place and emergency travel kits so you are prepared to respond should another disaster follow shortly after this one.

Seek medical evaluation and treatment for any injuries that occurred during the disaster.

YOUR CHECKLIST — HEAVY PRECIPITATION & FLOODING

Prepare For Primary Disaster Effects — Heavy Precipitation & Flooding

❑ Keep extra blankets in your vehicle;

❑ Plan several evacuation routes ahead of any disaster;

❑ In the event of a potential evacuation, ensure your vehicle is filled with gas;

❑ Update each of your emergency kits — add extra water, water-resistant and seasonal clothing for each person in your group, as well as several thick, waterproof zip-lock bags, and small candles for heat;

❑ Know how to turn off your utilities — gas, water and electric;

❑ Move sensitive and valuable items from your lower level; move furniture and other items as time allows;

❑ If you have time, attempt to block and divert potential floodwaters from entering your home.

Protect From Primary Disaster Effects — Heavy Precipitation & Flooding

❑ Follow alerts, and make sure children at schools and daycare centers are picked up;

❑ For a Flash Flood Warning:

    ❑ Stay at home unless you are in the direct path of the flood;

    ❑ When driving, move to high ground and stay there;

    ❑ Do not attempt to drive or walk through floodwaters;

    ❑ Listen to local news sources and check the Internet to determine when the Warning is over;

    ❑ Do not go near any floodwaters or standing water after the flood. It could be contaminated or electrically charged;

❑ For potential flooding of a flood plain or other location:

    ❑ Follow the news and weather in your area; where and when do they predict flooding;

    ❑ If authorities plan a "controlled" levee break to manage the floodwaters, plan to evacuate well before this break occurs;

    ❑ Turn off utilities before leaving;

    ❑ Check your evacuation routes before you leave to make sure you do not choose a route in danger from floodwaters;

    ❑ Evacuate with enough time to avoid the flood and no later than when authorities call for an evacuation; **Do Not Wait To Evacuate!**

❏ Evacuate well out of the flood area;

❏ Once you are on your way, let your local and long-distance contacts know your situation, who is with you, and what route you will take to evacuate;

❏ Call your contacts and let them know when you have safely reached your destination.

For actions after the disaster, see page 57.

Notes

Notes

Notes

Chapter 7: Extreme Heat & Wildfires

SCAN FOR CHAPTER OVERVIEW VIDEO

Extreme heat and wildfires are part of seasonal weather in the United States. They can occur anywhere, and are particularly dangerous to the very young and the elderly.

Periods of extreme heat can last weeks and are often called heat waves. Wildfires occur naturally and can start many ways, including from a lightning strike or a poorly tended campfire. High, shifting winds can cause the fire to grow and move unpredictably. A small brush fire or forest fire can grow into a very dangerous wildfire that quickly spreads across the countryside.

When you take the time to better understand and prepare for heat waves and wildfires, you will improve your ability to overcome their effects and reduce the chance of injury or death.

WHY SHOULD YOU BE CONCERNED?

Extreme heat and wildfires are severe weather disasters that can be deadly and destructive. Heat waves can affect tens of millions of people in a given year. Wildfires burn an average of 5 million acres every year. The 2011 North American Heat Wave was a deadly one that affected most of the United States east of the Mississippi River. At times, the heat index — a measure of the combined effects of the temperature and humidity — reached the equivalent of almost 130 degrees Fahrenheit. Considered nationally, this was the hottest heat wave in 75 years and the warmest year on record. This heat wave was also blamed for more than 25 deaths.

Regardless of where you live, these types of disasters can affect you. Even Alaska has seen injury and death from extreme heat and wildfires.

WHAT CAUSES EXTREME HEAT & WILDFIRES?

Extreme heat is described as heat more than 10 degrees above the average high for a region and lasting for several weeks or longer. It can be caused by a combination of high temperatures, low to high humidity but little rain, and a weather pattern that causes an air mass to stay over one area for a period of what could be weeks. Heat waves usually occur during the summer.

Wildfires are uncontrolled fires that typically start in the wilderness or countryside. They can occur in the summer, fall and winter. They become more likely when an extreme dry period occurs where there is significant vegetation that can dry out to fuel any fire.

However, you can prepare and protect from these extreme weather disasters and their effects.

DISASTER EFFECTS & HAZARDS

You will have to prepare for and protect from extreme heat, fire, smoke and reduced visibility. Hazards include dehydration, heat exhaustion and heat stroke. There is also an increased risk of landslides if, for example, a hilly area receives a significant amount of rainfall after it has been scoured by wildfire. Essential services, particularly power, could also be impacted as the demand for electricity to cool homes and businesses overwhelms the power grid, resulting in rolling brownouts or even blackouts.

The National Weather Service will issue extreme heat alerts, from the least dangerous, "Outlook," to the most dangerous, "Warning." The "Warning" alert carries the same meaning for extreme heat that it does for other weather-related disasters — significant danger from the named weather event. The levels are described in greater detail in the table below.

Excessive Heat Alert Levels:

Term	Description
Excessive Heat Outlook	Issued when the potential exists for an excessive heat event in the next 3 to 7 days.
Excessive Heat Watch	Issued when conditions are favorable for an excessive heat event in the next 12 to 48 hours.
Excessive Heat Advisory	Issued when an excessive heat event is occurring, is imminent, or has a very high probability of occurring, typically within the next 36 hours. Conditions can cause significant discomfort or inconvenience and, if caution is not taken, could lead to a threat to life and/ or property.
Excessive Heat Warning	Issued when an excessive heat event is occurring, is imminent, or has a very high probability of occurring, typically within the next 36 hours. Conditions pose a threat to life and/or property.

Source: NOAA website

The U.S. Department of Agriculture, U.S. Forest Service, publishes a National Fire Danger Rating for land in the federal park system. The National Fire Danger Rating System rates fire danger as follows: low, moderate, high, very high and extreme. This rating will help you gauge the danger from wildfire if you live near a national forest or you are planning on traveling to or through one of these forests. This rating will be posted along roads and entrances into the area. For other wildfire threats, listen to the news and radio, check the Internet, and listen for local alerts. If you are uncertain about the current danger from either extreme heat or wildfire, call the local authorities to get additional guidance.

PREPARE BEFORE EXTREME HEAT & WILDFIRES

In Chapter 2, we discussed primary disaster effects for heat waves and wildfires, so you know you can usually shelter-in-place from a heat wave but that you need to evacuate if you are in danger from a wildfire. Either way, plan to stay informed. If you have school-age children, find out the school policy regarding heat waves. Some schools do not have air-conditioning and will either cancel classes or shorten the school day during periods of extreme heat. Sign up for the school alert service so you can best respond to short notice changes.

Maintain your vehicle. Follow the guidance provided in Chapter 2. Wildfires can travel quickly and shift directions suddenly, so you must be prepared to evacuate with little warning. Make sure your vehicle has been checked and prepared for hot weather. If you own an older vehicle, consider keeping extra coolant and oil in the trunk. This gives you some ability to recharge fluids and try to avoid overheating your radiator and vehicle engine.

Update your emergency travel kit. Add extra water and sunscreen as well as light clothing, a hat, light gloves, a mask and good walking shoes for each person in your group.

At a minimum, you need to buy masks called "particulate respirators." They are usually labeled "NIOSH" and typically have "N95" or "P100" printed on them. Many hardware stores have this kind of mask.

Keep two blankets in each vehicle — these could be very important if you are caught in a wildfire.

Maintain Your Shelter-In-Place Location. Follow the guidance provided in Chapter 2. If you live or shelter in a home with several floors, you may need to rest or stay on the first floor or in the basement to stay cool. Your air-conditioning may work fine, but power outages are beyond your control.

If you live near a wooded area or in a location that may be threatened by wildfire, you need to prepare your home — your shelter-in-place location if it is somewhere other than your home — and the surrounding area. Where there are dead bushes or trees nearby, cut them down and remove them. Minimize possible fuel for a fire by moving anything that can burn, like a woodpile, away from the house. Plan to move porch and lawn furniture away from the house if the fire danger grows.

Update Your Emergency Shelter-In-Place Kit. Add extra water and sunscreen as well as light clothing, a hat, a mask like those in your emergency travel kit, light gloves and good walking shoes for each person in your group. Place a fire extinguisher in or near your shelter-in-place location so you can put out small fires that could start nearby in extremely dry weather. A garden hose and fire extinguisher can help you put out small fires. If you are trying to put out fires caused by embers from a wildfire, you are too close to the wildfire, and you need to evacuate!

PROTECT FROM EXTREME HEAT & WILDFIRES

An Extreme Heat Watch has been declared or very dry conditions in your region have led to the spread of wildfires. What do you do?

If you face a heat wave, sheltering-in-place is likely your best option, especially if you have air-conditioning and there are no warnings of planned power outages. If there are any preparations that you have not completed, like stocking up on extra water or removing dead trees and bushes from near your home or shelter location, do them now. A heat wave, by itself, is usually not enough to cause you to evacuate. Wildfires are a different matter. If you are in danger from a wildfire or you have limited options to evacuate and these routes may be threatened by wildfire, then you should evacuate quickly. With wildfires, you should always have several evacuation routes planned.

Stay Informed

Follow news and warnings regarding extreme heat alerts and wildfire outbreaks. Watch for alerts from school and daycare centers so you know if children will be released from school early or if the facility will be closed for a day or more. Call the authorities to get the locations of several heat-relief centers. A wildfire is one of the worst kinds of fires, moving suddenly and with great speed. If there is a danger from wildfire, you need to regularly check the news and Internet to avoid being surprised.

When you are traveling, rely on alerts, the Internet and your contacts to warn you if there is a potential problem with wildfires along your travel route or at a vacation destination. You should not intentionally travel through an area where there are wildfires unless it is an emergency. If it is an emergency, make sure your emergency travel kit is fully stocked and that you have at least two blankets in the vehicle. Let contacts know about your trip, when you leave, the route you are taking and when you expect to arrive at your destination.

Take Action

You are now in the middle of a heat wave or there are wildfires in your area. What do you do?

When you are experiencing a heat wave, try to limit the time you spend outside. If you must be outside, wear light clothing, including a long-sleeve shirt and a hat, and use sunscreen to help reduce the effects of direct sunlight. When the heat is this bad, though, it is better to stay in the shade or in an air-conditioned environment. Save lawn work for early or late in the day, drink a lot of water and avoid too much time in the direct sunlight. If you do not have air-conditioning, consider spending several hours each day in a public library or mall if they are air-conditioned.

Do not leave a child or pet in a locked vehicle. Even if the windows are slightly down, this still creates a dangerous heat build-up that can cause harm or even death. Make sure children and pets get extra water during a heat wave.

If you temporarily lose power, shelter in the coolest part of your home. If you have pets and the power outage lasts too long, you can call local contacts to see if you can stay with one of them. If you don't have pets, you can go to a heat-relief center. If you lose power and you do not know when it will be restored, you may have to evacuate. When deciding whether to stay or evacuate, remember that your safety and the safety of your family or group should be your first concern.

Heat waves can last for weeks. You cannot wait to treat heat injuries, like heat exhaustion and heat stroke, until after the heat wave is over. If someone has a heat injury, get the injured person into the shade and cool them with water and a wet cloth. Call emergency services for help. Go to http://emergency.cdc.gov/disasters/extremeheat/heat_guide.asp to learn more about heat injuries and how to treat them.

If you are experiencing drought conditions, any uncontrolled fire can be dangerous and could start a major fire or even a wildfire. If you grill out or burn debris, keep a fire extinguisher or connected garden hose nearby so you can stop a small fire from growing or spreading. Keep a watch on any fire until it is put out, and make sure the fire is out before leaving the location. If your area is experiencing a very dry period, don't do open-air burning, and keep any other fires small and contained.

You have been following the news, Internet and alerts from the authorities. You know there is a danger from wildfire. Listen for any change in the wildfire status that will cause you to evacuate immediately. Put any pets into a single room so you will not have to chase them around your home if you have to leave suddenly. Consider putting smaller animals into travel carriers if you are within 30 minutes of your planned evacuation time.

If you have time to safely take a few last-minute precautions before evacuating, consider doing the following at your home or shelter location: shut off the gas; close all exterior doors and windows, interior doors and any fireplace screens to reduce any draft; open fireplace dampers, close shutters and non-flammable blinds; take down flammable drapes and curtains. Your goal here is to reduce the chance of your home catching fire if a wild-fire reaches it.

It is better to leave before the authorities call for an evacuation or you see an actual fire coming toward you. If you wait until a wildfire is too close, you may not have time to gather your family or group to evacuate safely. Understand your evacuation route options. Which are open and have little, if any, fuel, like trees, to feed a wildfire? Which are rural roads with forest or brush filling each side of the road? Your danger is not just that the wildfire will reach or burn your shelter-in-place location, but that it will also overrun a key part of your evacuation route taking away a path to safety.

If your family or group live in multiple locations, be prepared for part of the group to evacuate on their own. Call your long-distance contact and let them know who is evacuating with you and what route you are taking. If others are evacuating, but separated from you, your long-distance contact can coordinate a safe place for you to meet.

If you cannot evacuate away from a wildfire, you are in a very dangerous situation and your best option is to seek protection from it.

If you are caught in your home, shelter together in the middle of the house. Cover your-selves with blankets and use your masks if smoke starts to get inside. Do not leave your shelter location until the wildfire is past.

You have a better chance to survive by staying in your vehicle than by trying to outrun a wildfire, so if you are caught in your vehicle, stay there. Park as far away from places with a lot of fuel, like heavy brush and dense forest, as you can. Roll up all windows and close all vents. Turn off your vehicle engine, lie down on the floor and cover yourself with one of the blankets you kept in your vehicle. Use your masks if smoke starts to get inside. Wait in your vehicle until the wildfire is past, even if it gets hot or smoky inside.

If you are caught outside, find an open area with as little fuel, like brush or trees, as pos-sible. If you have time to clear the area you will shelter in, do so. Shelter under whatever cover you can, like a coat or blanket. Wait until the wildfire is past.

Communicate

Once the heat wave is over or the wildfire has gone out, treat injuries within your abilities and seek medical assistance as needed. Inspect your shelter-in-place location to ensure it is still safe to stay in. Put out any embers on or near the shelter if you could not evacuate away from the wildfire. If you did evacuate, listen to the news and check the Internet. Have the authorities given permission to return to the area?

Does your shelter or home, if they are not in the same location, still have access to the services you need, like power, water and food? Wait until it is safe to return. Once you return, call your local and long-distance contacts to let them know how you are doing, then restock your emergency kits so you are prepared for the next disaster whenever it comes.

YOUR CHECKLIST —
EXTREME HEAT & WILDFIRES

Prepare For Primary Disaster Effects — Extreme Heat & Wildfires

❑ Keep coolant and oil with an older vehicle;

❑ Update each of your emergency kits — add extra water, sunscreen and two blankets, as well as a "particulate respirator" mask for each person;

❑ Store a fire extinguisher in or near your shelter location;

❑ Remove wildfire fuel sources like dead trees or bushes, and shift fuel sources like woodpiles away from your home and shelter locations.

Protect From Primary Disaster Effects — Extreme Heat & Wildfires

❑ Follow alerts, and make sure children at schools and daycare centers are picked up;

❑ For a heat wave, limit the time you spend outside:

  ❑ Save lawn work for early or late in the day, drink a lot of water and avoid too much time in direct sunlight;

  ❑ When you are outside, wear light clothing, including a long-sleeve shirt and a hat, and use sunscreen to help reduce the effects of direct sunlight;

  ❑ Spend time in an air-conditioned building to cool down; visit a public library, heat-relief center or mall if you don't have air-conditioning;

  ❑ **Do Not** leave children or pets inside a locked vehicle;

  ❑ Get emergency services assistance if there is a heat injury; cool the injured person until expert help arrives.

❑ When your area is very dry, keep any fires small, contained and controlled; do not leave any fire unattended, and stay until it is out; **Do Not** do open-air burning;

❑ If there is a danger from wildfire, make your final evacuation preparations:

  ❑ Put any pets into a single room, and consider putting small pets into carriers if you are within 30 minutes of your evacuation time;

  ❑ Prepare your home or shelter location: shut off the gas; close all exterior doors and windows, interior doors and fireplace screens; open fireplace dampers; close shutters and non-flammable blinds; take down flammable drapes and curtains;

❑ Check your evacuation routes before you leave to make sure you do not choose a route in danger from a wildfire;

❑ Evacuate before you see the wildfire and no later than when authorities call for an evacuation; **Do Not Wait To Evacuate!**

❑ Once you are on your way, let your local and long-distance contacts know your situation, who is with you, and what route you will take to evacuate;

❏ If you get caught by a wildfire, you are in extreme danger, so protect as follows:

   ❏ Shelter together *in the middle of your home;* cover yourselves with blankets; use your masks if smoke starts to get inside;

   ❏ *In a vehicle,* park on the road as far from dense forest, heavy brush and other large fuel sources as possible; roll up all windows; close all vents; turn off your vehicle engine; lay down on the floor and cover yourselves with a blanket; use your masks if needed;

   ❏ *If you are outside,* find an open area with as little fuel as possible; clear any fuel from the area you will shelter in if there is time; seek cover under a coat or blanket;

❏ Do not leave your shelter until the wildfire is past, and then check it to make sure all embers are out.

For actions after the disaster, see page 57.

Notes

Notes

Notes

Chapter 8: Earthquakes

SCAN FOR CHAPTER OVERVIEW VIDEO

An earthquake is the violent shaking or movement of the earth's surface. You will not be able to feel the vast majority of earthquakes that occur because they are so small. Some earthquakes can only be felt locally, while large earthquakes can cause great destruction and can be felt from hundreds of miles away. You may not live in an area where earthquakes are common, but you can still be vulnerable. Earthquakes can occur in many places that are not known for earthquake activity.

Your planning and preparation will help you protect yourself and others if you find yourself in the middle of an earthquake.

WHY SHOULD YOU BE CONCERNED?

According to the United States Geological Survey, 30 of 50 states are likely to experience seismic activity. Over the last decade, the U.S. has averaged over 3,500 earthquakes a year. We can actually feel more than 400 quakes in any given year. Although deaths due to

earthquakes are rare in the U.S. (only two from 2000 to 2010), there have been over 5 million earthquake-related deaths across the globe during the same time period. The primary reason there have been so few deaths in the U.S. is not because of our high standards for building construction, though this has helped, but rather it is because we have not had a large, devastating earthquake during this period while other countries have.

In 1994, Northridge, California, was hit by a magnitude 6.7 earthquake. There was no significant earthquake activity before the Northridge quake struck. It killed 60 people, injured some 7,000 and damaged or destroyed more than 40,000 buildings. As bad as this earthquake was, it is far from the most powerful earthquake that has hit the U.S. in the last few hundred years. In late 1811 to early 1812, three very strong earthquakes occurred near New Madrid, Missouri. One was estimated at magnitude 7 to 8. It was felt as far away as Maine and Canada, and it rang church bells in Charleston, South Carolina. There was very little loss of life because the area was sparsely populated. If an earthquake of this magnitude struck the same place today, it could result in the most destructive U.S. earthquake in modern times. There is no doubt the U.S. will experience large earthquakes in the future — it is a matter of when and where they will occur.

WHAT CAUSES EARTHQUAKES?

An earthquake is the shaking of the ground caused by volcanic activity or the abrupt shifting of rock along lines, or fractures, in the Earth's surface. These fractures are called faults. Faults are found near weaknesses in the Earth's surface, like the boundary between two plates or an area where the Earth's surface thinned and weakened in the distant past. The outer layer of the earth is actually a series of large plates that move very slowly through time. The boundary between these plates is a place where stress builds up as the plates slide past each other. Rock does not slide past other rock easily. When the stress grows too large, the plates move, releasing this stress. This release can cause earthquakes and help trigger volcanic eruptions, which are discussed in more detail in Chapter 9.

The U.S. is home to a number of large fault zones. A fault zone is a series of faults that spread over what may be hundreds of miles. A well-known example would be the San Andreas fault zone on the West Coast. Though less well known, the New Madrid fault zone is the most active U.S. fault zone east of the Rocky Mountains. It runs from southern Illinois down into Arkansas, while extending into Kentucky and Tennessee. Fault zones are places where earthquakes occur more frequently.

There is no accurate way to predict earthquakes at the present time. While some large earthquakes may occur after what seems like a build-up from smaller earthquake activity, this is not always the case. In the 1994 Northridge quake, there was no warning from an increase in earthquake activity. We are better able to predict where an earthquake will occur. If you live in one of the fault zones discussed earlier in this chapter, you are more likely to experience earthquake activity.

DISASTER EFFECTS & HAZARDS

You will have to prepare for and protect from earthquake effects, including falling debris, landslides and mudslides, and possibly a tsunami. Some of the hazards that can be associated with earthquakes include: flooding; wild fires; damage and destruction of critical infrastructure like bridges, roads and dams; and possibly industrial accidents like a poisonous gas release due to building damage.

One way the energy release of an earthquake can be measured is using the Richter Scale. As magnitude goes up, the energy release increases dramatically. Each whole number increase of 1.0 equals a 30 times increase in energy release. For example, a magnitude 5.0 earthquake releases about 30 times more energy than a magnitude 4.0 earthquake. This should help explain why the death toll and damage from strong or major earthquakes is so much worse than that caused by minor or light earthquakes.

Magnitude	Class	Effects	Est. Annually
1.0–2.9	Minor	Rarely felt.	
3.0–3.9	Minor	Felt noticeably or by a few on upper floors of buildings. May not be recognized as an earthquake.	900,000
4.0–4.9	Light	Felt by those indoors.	30,000
5.0–5.9	Moderate	Felt by all and easily recognized as an earthquake. Slight damage to well-constructed buildings. Considerable damage to poorly constructed buildings.	500
6.0–6.9	Strong	Felt by all and easily recognized as an earthquake. Strong earthquakes have a wide range of effects. Total to partial collapse of buildings is possible, depending on construction. Many small buildings will shift on their foundations and walls can be thrown out of plumb.	100
>7.0	Major–Great*	Felt by all and easily recognized as an earthquake. Objects thrown into the air. A wide range of effects is likely throughout the region. Potential for total collapse of masonry and wood frame structures, bridges collapse and roads destroyed. Significant damage to well-constructed buildings.	20+

*Earthquakes measuring 8.0 or greater on the Richter Scale are considered "Great" earthquakes and are expected at a rate of one every five to 10 years.

PREPARE BEFORE EARTHQUAKES

You may not have any warning before an earthquake occurs. Whether you live in a high-risk area, like the California coast, or you live in a place where earthquakes are rare, preparation now gives you a better chance to avoid injury or worse if an earthquake occurs.

Maintain your vehicle and emergency travel kit following the guidance in Chapter 2. Select your shelter-in-place location for its ability to withstand an earthquake. Prepare this location and your home so that heavy objects are close to the floor, and pictures and other wall hangings are not positioned over your seats. If possible, add a sturdy piece of furniture, like a table, that you can shelter under to protect from falling debris and objects. Build your emergency kit and store it in your shelter-in-place location. Keep a fire extinguisher and protective coverings, like sleeping bags and thick blankets, in your shelter location. Identify other furniture around your house that you could shelter under if you are not very close to your shelter location when the earthquake occurs. Talk to your children, tell them what to do if there is an earthquake, and practice responding to an earthquake with them.

Discuss how you will communicate with your family or group. Plan to stay informed using radio, TV and the Internet. Subscribe to e-mail and text alerts for your area. Create a notebook that shows evacuation routes and pre-approved evacuation centers in your area, but be prepared to change your plans because a large earthquake can damage or destroy many of the roads and evacuation centers you plan to use. Contact your local community and county offices to learn about planning resources and ways to better prepare for an earthquake. Check with your place of work to learn about any guidance they provide on ways to protect an employee from the effects of an earthquake. Choose a place where you can shelter at work if an earthquake should strike during the workday.

PROTECT FROM EARTHQUAKES

Stay Informed

While we cannot predict when an earthquake will occur, the authorities in some states, like California, are working to create an earthquake warning system. This system could give enough warning to allow a parent to grab nearby children and get to the shelter-in-place location before the earthquake effects strike. There could also be the danger of a tsunami if there is a large earthquake beneath the ocean floor near your coast. Listen to the radio, TV and Internet and move to your shelter-in-place location or evacuate, based on the type of danger you face. You will learn more about tsunamis in Chapter 10.

Take Action

Whether an earthquake comes after a number of smaller tremors or it suddenly occurs, take action quickly. Everyone should seek shelter immediately. Parents may need to get to small children and help them shelter. The quicker you do can do this, the better the chance of avoiding an injury, or worse. If you do not have time to get to your shelter location, get to the best cover at hand.

If you are indoors during an earthquake, use the rule "Drop, Cover and Hold-on": drop to the floor; take cover under sturdy furniture such as a desk or table; cover yourself with thick blankets or sleeping bags to protect from debris; hold on to ensure you remain covered and protected from falling debris; stay away from outside walls, windows and doors.

If you are in bed when a quake hits, stay there unless your bed is under a heavy light fixture. Protect your head with a pillow. Only shelter in a doorway if it is sturdy and no better protection is available. Stay away from glass, windows, walls and any furniture or fixtures that could fall. Do not attempt to use an elevator or stairs or try to leave the building during the earthquake. Research shows that many earthquake-related injuries occur when people try to evacuate a building during an earthquake.

If you are outdoors during an earthquake, stay there. Move away from buildings, utility wires, signs and streetlights. As a good rule of thumb, move away from anything that might turn into falling debris.

If you are in your vehicle during an earthquake, stay there. Stop the vehicle as quickly as safety permits. Do not stop under or near overpasses, buildings, signs, trees and utility wires to avoid possible falling debris. Once the earthquake is over, drive cautiously. Avoid driving on roads, bridges, overpasses and ramps that may have been damaged by the earthquake.

Do not attempt to run into a building during or immediately after an earthquake. Many injuries and deaths have occurred when people ran into a building immediately after an earthquake and got hit by falling debris. Wait for the earthquake to end and for debris to stop falling before leaving the safety of your cover. Earthquakes typically last less than a minute.

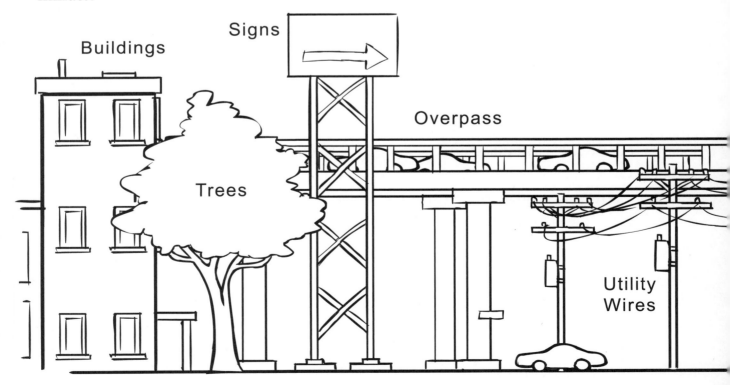

Communicate

If you are trapped under debris, stay calm. Cover your mouth with a handkerchief or cloth. Do not shout or scream, or light a match. Try to avoid breathing in the dust around you. You may be able to use your cell phone to try to call for help. Whether you have a cell phone or not, tap a pipe or wall at regular intervals to alert rescue crews to your location. Once you are rescued, let your long-distance contacts know your status and try to rejoin your family or group.

If you are not trapped under debris, check for and treat injuries as best you can. Call your long-distance contacts and let them know your status. If needed, get their help contacting emergency medical services if anyone has a life-threatening or serious injury or medical condition. Examine your shelter for damage and make sure it is safe to stay there, even in the short term.

Listen to the radio, check the Internet and call local contacts to identify what hazards you may have to protect from. A large earthquake can create many hazards, from fire and flooding to downed power lines and gas leaks. In addition to these hazards, you could have lost access to essential and very important services like food, water, power and emergency services. You will have to decide whether or not to evacuate if these services may not be restored before you use up the supplies in your emergency kits.

Whether you choose to stay or evacuate, let your local and long-distance contacts know your plans and seek medical evaluation and treatment for any injuries.

YOUR CHECKLIST — EARTHQUAKES

Prepare For Primary Disaster Effects — Earthquakes

❏ Build your emergency kits, and store a fire extinguisher and protective coverings, like sleeping bags and thick blankets, in your shelter location;

❏ Prepare this location and your home so that heavy objects are close to the floor and pictures and other wall hangings are not positioned over your seats;

❏ Identify furniture, like a table or desk, which you could shelter under if you had only moments to respond to an earthquake;

❏ Talk to your children so they understand what to do if there is an earthquake;

❏ Discuss how you will communicate with your family or group.

Protect From Primary Disaster Effects — Earthquakes

❏ Seek shelter immediately;

❏ If indoors, Drop, Cover and Hold-On; Protect your head;

   ❏ Stay under furniture, even if it moves, to avoid injury from falling debris;

   ❏ Stay away from outside walls, windows and doors;

   ❏ Do not attempt to leave the building during the earthquake;

❏ If outdoors, move away from buildings, utility wires, signs and streetlights;

❏ If in your vehicle, stop it as quickly and safely as possible and stay in it;

   ❏ Avoid stopping under or near overpasses, buildings, signs, trees and utility wires;

❏ If trapped under debris, cover your mouth with a cloth or handkerchief;

   ❏ Do not disturb the dust around you, shout or scream, or light a match;

   ❏ If your cell phone works, use it to call for help;

   ❏ Tap a pipe or wall at regular intervals to alert rescuers to your location.

For actions after the disaster, see page 57.

Notes

Notes

Notes

Chapter 9: Volcanoes

SCAN FOR CHAPTER OVERVIEW VIDEO

A volcano begins as a vertical shaft or opening from the earth's interior through its crust to the surface. Molten rock, called magma, rises through this opening onto the earth's surface, spreading and cooling, then repeating this process until magma no longer follows this particular path to the surface.

These eruptions — some quiet and some not — can build a hill or mountain over time. Some eruptions might cause the slow, steady flow of lava, while other eruptions could throw hot ash and rock thousands of feet into the air when the volcano explodes with the force of a small nuclear weapon.

If you do not live in an area with a live volcano, you are much less likely to be directly impacted by some of the effects from an eruption, but that is no guarantee you will not be affected by the volcano. One effect, an ash cloud, can travel great distances. Your planning and preparation will help you to protect from these effects and reduce the chance of injury.

WHY SHOULD YOU BE CONCERNED?

Volcanoes can erupt quietly or with a great explosion, producing lava and mudflows, clouds of ash and poisonous gas, and even hurling rocks for miles. They can be found on land and on the ocean floor. They are most common along the West Coast of the United States and in Alaska, but there are some found in the western half of the U.S. A major volcanic eruption can produce a large ash cloud that wind can carry for hundreds of miles or more, dropping ash across cities, roads and fields, as well as interfering with air travel.

Mount St. Helens, in the state of Washington, is one of more than a dozen active or dormant volcanoes in the Cascade Range. This is a mountain range extending from southern British Columbia through Washington and Oregon into Northern California. In May 1980, a 5.1-magnitude earthquake shook Mt. St. Helens, causing a very large avalanche along its northern slope. This effectively uncorked the bottle as the pressure inside the volcano then blew out part of the north face of the mountain in what is called a lateral explosion. This explosion and the primary disaster effects that followed killed more than 50 people, destroyed hundreds of homes and more than 40 bridges, and leveled trees over a 230-square-mile area. Ash climbed 12 miles into the air and fell over the Pacific Northwest and beyond. The ash spread eastward, reaching Idaho in three hours, and eventually spread to cover parts of 11 states. In little more than three hours, ash reached Spokane, Washington, reducing visibility to 10 feet, and falling to a depth of half an inch. Ash from the eruption was found in Denver the day after the event.

The most dangerous kind of volcano is called a supervolcano. These are very large volcanoes that can cause devastation and damaging effects across a thousand miles or more. Some of these volcanoes have erupted, putting so much ash into the atmosphere that they actually caused the earth's average temperature to drop for years. The U.S. is home to at least two of these supervolcanoes: the Yellowstone Caldera and the Valles Caldera in New Mexico. Old Faithful, one of the many geysers at Yellowstone National Park, is heated by magma below the park's surface. It serves to remind us that the Yellowstone Caldera is not an extinct volcano, just one that sleeps lightly.

WHAT CAUSES VOLCANOES?

A volcano is created by pressure from below the earth's surface. When this pressure reaches a critical point, it fractures part of the rock keeping it in place, and an eruption occurs. Think of the volcano like a balloon. The surface of the balloon stretches as more and more air gets pushed into it. When the balloon breaks, the air is suddenly released. Now, take that image and replace the balloon and air with a mountain and magma; the greater the pressure buildup, the greater the chance of a violent eruption when the rock finally ruptures.

Many volcanoes form at the boundaries between the earth's plates. The outer layer of the earth is actually a series of large plates that move very slowly through time. The boundary between these plates is a place where stress builds up as the plates slide past each other, or one plate forces the other plate down into the earth's interior. Release of this stress can cause earthquakes and help trigger volcanic eruptions.

Some volcanoes can form where the earth's crust stretches or thins. Hot molten rock under great pressure rises up from deep in the earth, following a weakness in the earth's crust above it — the area that is stretched or thinned. These places are called "hot spots." Some volcanoes form over these hot spots. On land, we see the hills and mountains formed by volcanoes, but we rarely see the volcanoes that are formed on the ocean's floor. Hawaii is believed to have been formed from hot-spot volcanoes over millions of years. Mauna Loa in Hawaii may be the tallest volcano on earth, stretching some 29,000 feet from its base on the ocean floor to its top, about 13,000 feet above sea level.

DISASTER EFFECTS & HAZARDS

You will have to prepare for and protect from effects, including lava and mudflows, clouds of ash and poisonous gas, and hot rock thrown or ejected from the volcano. Some of the hazards that come with these effects include fires started by lava and hot rock, reduced visibility due to ash settling out the air, engine shutdown when ash clogs filters, problems breathing because of the ash in the air, and even flash floods. Very heavy ash falls can occur near a large volcano. They may need to be swept off roofs to prevent collapse from the weight of the ash and reduce the chance of fire. Some volcanic explosions can blast part of the mountain out sideways. The pressure wave created by this blast can flatten a forest as well as damage or destroy nearby buildings and structures.

The U.S. Geological Survey (USGS) monitors active and potentially active volcanoes in the United States. They use the following alert levels to identify the potential danger associated with particular volcanoes.

Volcano Alert Levels:

Term	Description
Normal	Volcano is in typical background, non-eruptive state or, after a change from a higher level, volcanic activity has ceased and volcano has returned to non-eruptive background state.
Advisory	Volcano is exhibiting signs of elevated unrest above known background level or, after a change from a higher level, volcanic activity has decreased significantly but continues to be closely monitored for possible renewed increase.
Watch	Volcano is exhibiting heightened or escalating unrest with increased potential of eruption, timeframe uncertain OR Eruption is underway but poses limited hazards.
Warning	Hazardous eruption is imminent, underway, or suspected.

Fact Sheet, USGS Alert Notification System for Volcanic Activity

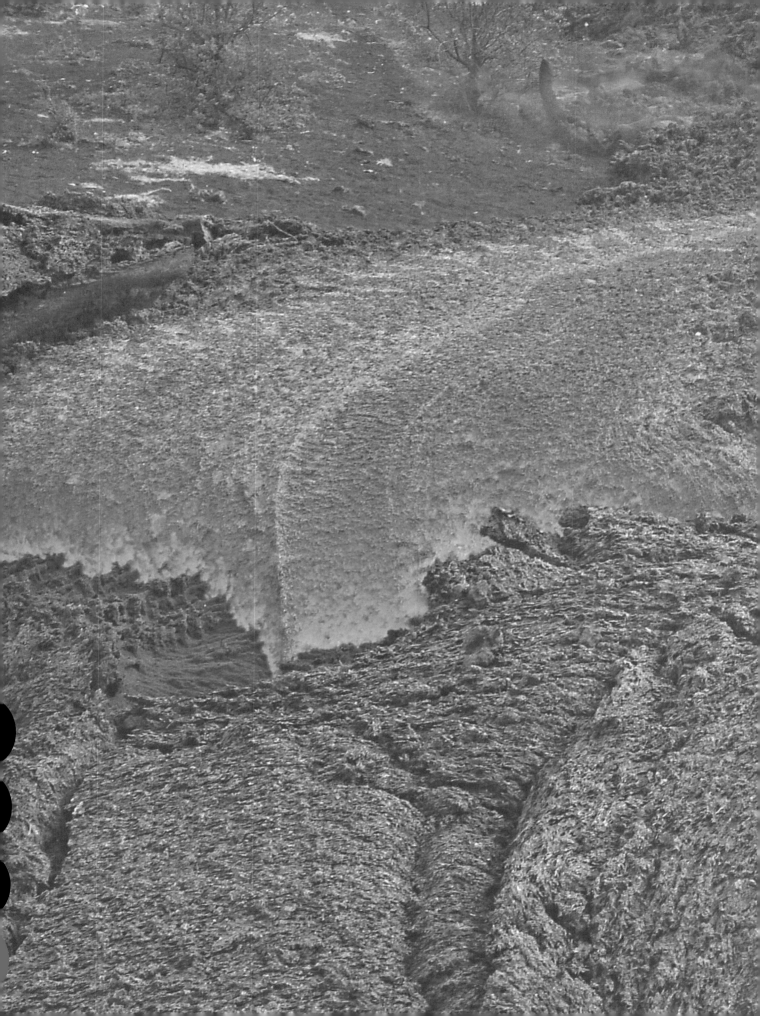

There is an aviation color code used to identify the danger a volcanic eruption poses to flights downwind of ash clouds. Green is normal or no danger, through Yellow and Orange, to Red; Red means that there is or may be a significant ash release by the volcano. Wind can carry these ash clouds thousands of miles from their source. Jets will be rerouted to avoid the ash clouds because ash can clog and shut down aircraft engines.

PREPARE BEFORE VOLCANIC ERUPTIONS

A potential or actual volcanic eruption in the United States will usually come with some advance warning. In the U.S., the U.S. Geological Survey will declare a volcano advisory, watch or warning. If you live near an active or dormant volcano, make sure you watch the news and Internet for any increase in volcanic activity. Plan to stay informed. If anyone is in school, check with the school so you understand their policy regarding early release or cancellation of school due to the increased threat, or actual occurrence, of a volcanic eruption. Make sure you sign up for any alert service the school has. Discuss who will pick up a child if the school closes early. Now, focus your preparations on your vehicle and your shelter-in-place location.

Maintain your vehicle by following the guidance provided in Chapter 2. If you live near an active or dormant volcano, you must be prepared to evacuate immediately. Fill up with gas as soon as there is any increase in volcanic activity beyond what is normal for the volcano you live near. Your vehicle is your best chance to evacuate away from effects that you cannot shelter from, like lava and fire.

Update your emergency travel kit. Regardless of the time of year, you need to add a long-sleeve shirt, pants, a season-appropriate hat, gloves, thick socks and good walking shoes or boots for each person in your group. Each person will also need eye protection, like a pair of goggles, as well as several disposable breathing masks. Pack scarfs or cotton t-shirts to make improvised covers for your nose and mouth if you do not have enough breathing masks. Refill your kit with water bottles, snack food and high-calorie food bars.

Maintain your shelter-in-place location by following the guidance provided in Chapter 2. If you live near an active or dormant volcano, you can prepare your shelter-in-place location to withstand some of the effects, like an ash cloud or heavy ash settling on your roof. Your efforts to weatherize your home to protect from severe winter weather will keep out most ash just as well. You may need to seal your garage door with plastic and duct tape to reduce the amount of ash that gets in. This will make it easier for you to prevent ash from clogging your air filter and stopping your vehicle's engine. Remember, you cannot shelter-in-place from some effects, like fire or lava. You will have to evacuate if these primary disaster effects threaten your shelter location.

Update your emergency shelter-in-place kit. Add in a long-sleeve shirt, pants, a season-appropriate hat, gloves, thick socks and good walking shoes or boots for each person in your group. This becomes even more important for those who will shelter away from their

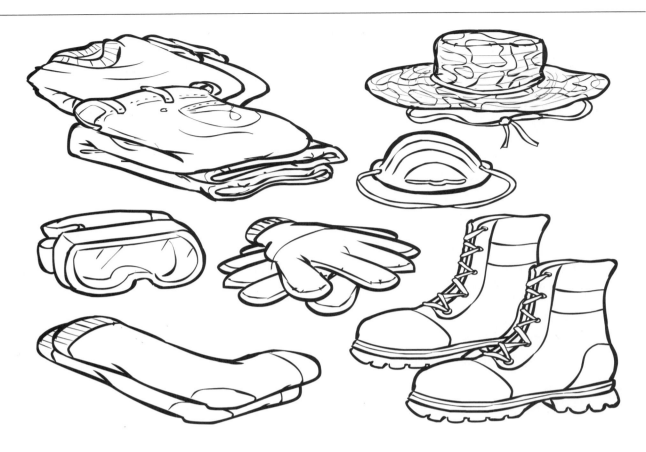

homes. Store at least one metal snow shovel near or in your shelter location. You can use this to shovel ash off the roof if you are concerned that the ash may cause your roof to collapse or that it is a fire hazard. Do not use a plastic shovel, because the ash could be corrosive and hot enough to damage or ruin the shovel after little use. Place a fire extinguisher in or near your shelter-in-place location so you can put out small fires that hot ash may start there. A garden hose and fire extinguisher can help you put out small fires. If the risk of fire is growing or you cannot continue to put out the fires at your shelter-in-place location, evacuate!

PROTECT FROM VOLCANIC ERUPTIONS

Volcanic activity has increased and the Volcano Alert "Advisory" has changed to a "Watch." Do you stay or do you evacuate? To answer this question, you need to know how far away you are from the volcano that may erupt. According to the Federal Emergency Management Agency (FEMA), the primary danger area is a 20-mile radius around a volcano. There is still the danger that some effects, like an ash cloud, will travel hundreds of miles or more, impacting anyone downwind from the volcano. This is "Watch," which means the danger level has increased significantly. If the alert had been a "Warning," it would mean that a dangerous eruption was imminent, if not already occurring.

Stay Informed

Follow news of the volcano alert. How quickly can everyone gather if the group needs to evacuate? Watch for alerts from schools and daycare centers so you know if children will need to be picked up early. If you are within 20 miles of the volcano, consider evacuating as quickly as you can. If the volcano quiets back down and the threat of an eruption is gone, you can always return home. If you wait until the "Warning" is declared or an actual eruption occurs, you may not have time to gather your family or group and evacuate safely. If you evacuate after the "Warning" is declared, you will likely become part of a crowd evacuation, reducing your evacuation route options and the speed at which you can leave the area.

The ash from a very large volcano can cover thousands of square miles and more. Krakatoa, a volcanic island between Sumatra and Java, exploded in 1883 with an estimated force of 200 megatons, which is equal to 200 million tons of dynamite. The ash column went 50 miles into the air and spread to cover some 800,000 square miles. The ash was said to burn clothing on people as far as 50 miles away. If you wait until you are impacted by an ash cloud before you try to evacuate, it may already be too late. The ash can clog your air filter, causing your vehicle's engine to stop.

If you are traveling, rely on alerts, the Internet and your contacts to let you know if there is a problem with your travel route or destination. Many people do not listen to the radio when they travel, so it is especially important that you tell your contacts about your travel plans so they can warn you if there is trouble. Avoid not just the immediate area where a volcano alert "Watch" or "Warning" has been given, but also avoid the area downwind of the potential or actual volcanic eruption. Volcanic ash can travel great distances, especially if the eruption puts large amounts of ash miles above the earth's surface. If you are flying, contact your airline to see if the volcanic activity will interfere with your travel plans.

Be prepared for the "Watch" to become a "Warning." If you live near a live volcano and you chose not to evacuate beforehand, do not hesitate to gather your family or group and evacuate now. Some volcano effects can travel very quickly and you do not want to race a flash flood from suddenly melted snow to reach a bridge you must cross so you can safely leave the area.

Take Action

A Volcano Alert "Warning" has been announced for your area. A volcanic eruption may be about to occur or it may have already started. Gather your family or group. Call your long-distance contacts and get their help to coordinate the pick up of any children from schools and daycare, as well as adults that may not have transportation. Then evacuate.

If someone is too far away to join you before you evacuate, they should evacuate from their location. Anyone separated from the group should coordinate with your long-distance contacts and let them know where they will evacuate to and whether or not they will try to meet up with the group at a safe place along your evacuation route. Follow any evacuation instructions from the authorities; they may be aware of roads and bridges that can no longer be used because of damage from primary disaster effects.

When you evacuate, move to higher ground and avoid roads in valleys and low-lying areas near the eruption. Some of the volcanic eruption effects will move the same way water would. Travel on higher ground helps you to avoid mud, landslides, flash floods and lava, for example. Be careful crossing bridges near the eruption site so you are not caught on a bridge when an effect, like a mudslide, hits it.

If your vehicle is disabled by volcanic debris or falling ash, leave the vehicle, grab your emergency travel kit and head to higher ground. Put on your long-sleeve shirt, pants, hat, gloves and mask if there is a danger from falling ash. Watch for smoke from fires and move away from the eruption site and any fires you can see. Volcanoes can throw hot rocks and ash miles from the actual eruption location. You may have to try to avoid fires in front of you as well as behind you.

You can gather at your shelter-in-place location if you live far enough away from the eruption that there is no danger your shelter will be impacted by primary disaster effects. Follow the news and Internet to listen for warnings from the authorities about danger from

falling ash. Periodically check your shelter and verify that the falling ash has not started any fires. Take extra care if you have been living in drought conditions. With the increased danger from fire, consider trying to wet down your shelter's roof and walls, as well as any trees and shrubs near your location. This will reduce the chance of fire. If you cannot control and put out any fires that start or the fire danger becomes too dangerous, evacuate!

Communicate

When the eruption is over, listen to the news and check the Internet. Have the authorities given permission to return to the area impacted by the eruption? Volcanoes and the earthquakes that accompany them may have damaged facilities that provide power and water, for example. You do not want to return until the necessary services have been restored to the area. Check with your local contacts, as they may have specific information about your neighborhood and available services that could influence your decision to return or wait.

If you did not evacuate, check your shelter for damage and verify that you have access to essential services as well as other services you need. Call your local and long-distance contacts to let them know your status. Restock your shelter-in-place and emergency travel kits so you are prepared to respond should another disaster follow shortly after this one.

Seek medical evaluation and treatment for any injuries that occurred during the disaster.

YOUR CHECKLIST — VOLCANOES

Prepare For Primary Disaster Effects — Volcanoes

❑ Update your emergency kits with additional supplies;

❑ Add a long-sleeve shirt, pants, a season-appropriate hat, gloves, thick socks and good walking shoes or boots for each person in your group;

❑ Add eye protection, like a pair of goggles, as well as disposable breathing masks for each person; use scarfs or cotton t-shirts for improvised breathing masks;

❑ Weatherize your home just as you would to protect from cold winter weather. Be prepared to seal your garage door with plastic and duct tape;

❑ Store at least one metal snow shovel and fire extinguisher near or in your shelter location.

Protect From Primary Disaster Effects — Volcanoes

❑ Fill your vehicle with gas before a "Warning" is issued;

❑ Follow alerts, and make sure children at schools and daycare are picked up.

❑ *If you need to evacuate:*

    ❑ Put on your long-sleeve shirt and pants, and keep your hat, gloves and mask nearby;

    ❑ Account for all people and pets in the group;

    ❑ Call your long-distance contacts to tell them you are evacuating and the route you are taking;

    ❑ Check the radio and Internet, and talk to your long-distance contacts before you leave and as you are evacuating so you can respond to any identified problems with your original evacuation route.

❑ *If you shelter-in-place:*

    ❑ Call your local and long-distance contacts to let them know your shelter location and that you are staying;

    ❑ Consider wetting down your shelter and nearby trees and shrubs;

    ❑ Periodically check your shelter and the surrounding area to identify any fires;

    ❑ Listen for local alerts and look for signs of fires or other hazards;

    ❑ Evacuate if your shelter location cannot protect you from these hazards;

    ❑ Talk regularly with your local and long-distance contacts. Let them know about any changes in your status, evaluate any new dangers they identify, and decide whether to stay or evacuate based on the new information.

For actions after the disaster, see page 57.

Notes

Notes

Notes

Chapter 10: Tsunamis

SCAN FOR CHAPTER OVERVIEW VIDEO

A tsunami is a series of waves created by an underwater disturbance. This disturbance can take many forms, including an underwater earthquake, a meteorite strike or a major landslide into the ocean. The resulting waves travel quickly in deep water but appear to have very little height. When these waves reach shallow water, they slow and can increase dramatically in height.

Large tsunamis can inundate coastal areas with water, traveling miles inland where the land is flat and close to sea level in height. Tsunamis can affect islands, coastal areas and even the shorelines of large lakes or inland seas. Even if you do not live near a coast or a large body of water, you can still be affected if you travel to, or vacation in, these locations.

Your planning and preparation will help you to protect from the effects of a tsunami and reduce the chance of injury or death.

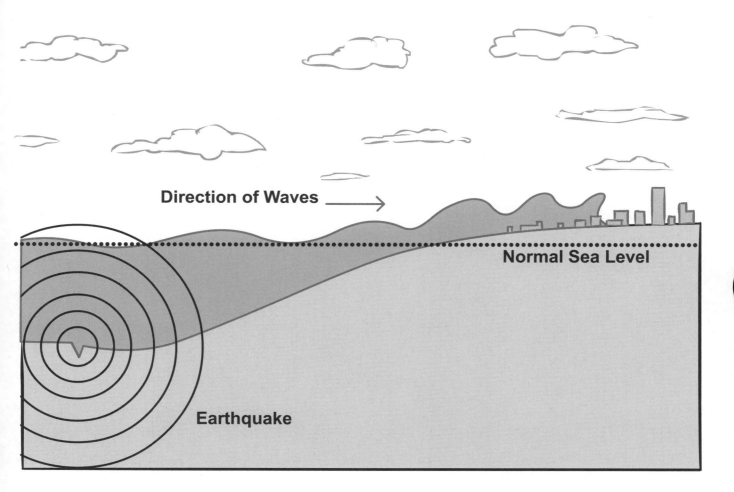

Direction of Waves ⟶

Normal Sea Level

Earthquake

WHY SHOULD YOU BE CONCERNED?

Tsunamis can occur with very little warning. They travel at speeds approaching 600 mph in deep water and do not slow down significantly until they reach the shallow water often associated with a coastal area. When they reach shallow water, they slow down to speeds of 40-plus mph and climb up toward the shoreline, revealing their true height. Sometimes, the water will appear to quickly move away from the shore like a receding tide, but far too fast to be normal, and it's not. This is one of the signs of the impending arrival of a tsunami. If you see it, evacuate to higher ground immediately and do not stop until you are much higher up or miles farther from shore, preferably both. Tsunamis can travel for thousands of miles across open water and still pose a serious danger to the coastlines of multiple continents.

On March 11, 2011, a magnitude 9.0 undersea earthquake occurred about 80 miles east of Sendai, Japan. This earthquake, called the Great Eastern Japan Earthquake, moved parts of northeastern Japan almost 8 feet closer to North America and caused a massive tsunami to spread across the Pacific Ocean. In Japan, this tsunami reached a height of more than 130 feet in places, overtopping many of the tsunami seawalls erected to protect from this type of event. In some places along the coast, the tsunami traveled almost 6 miles inland. The earthquake and resulting tsunami killed more than an estimated 18,000 people, damaged or destroyed more than 180,000 buildings, and helped to cause a nuclear accident and radiation release at the Fukushima Daiichi nuclear power plant.

A tsunami "Warning" was sent out across the Pacific and to all bordering land masses. Authorities in the U.S. issued a tsunami "Warning" for most of the California coast, all of Oregon and the western part of Alaska. The tsunami traveled more than 5,000 miles to reach Oregon and California, where tsunami surge topping 8 feet in height damaged harbors and docks.

As terrible as this event was, this century began with an even more deadly tsunami. On December 26, 2004, the Indian Ocean Earthquake occurred off the west coast of Sumatra, Indonesia. It was the third-largest earthquake since 1900, with a recorded magnitude of 9.0 to 9.3. This event caused a massive tsunami to spread out across the Indian Ocean and beyond. In places, it reached a height of almost 100 feet when it came on shore. The estimated death toll from this tsunami exceeded 300,000 people, concentrated in 14 of the countries bordering the Indian Ocean. Among the dead were more than 1,000 people vacationing from Europe.

WHAT CAUSES TSUNAMIS?

A tsunami can be caused by a major disturbance to a large body of water. Think of the ocean like a cup of water. Even though the water level is below the rim of the cup, when you bump the cup hard enough, the water inside will splash out. Now, replace the water and cup with the ocean and the earth's surface holding it. In a large body of water, a tsunami could be triggered by an earthquake or seaquake, which is an underwater earthquake; a major landslide or glacier calving, which is when a large part of a glacier breaks off and falls into the water; or even a large meteorite hitting the water's surface. If the trigger event bumps the "cup" hard enough, it could generate a tsunami that travels out across the water, away from the trigger event. The key for the formation of a tsunami is for a large amount of water to be displaced, or moved, by the trigger event.

We have already discussed in previous chapters how earthquakes can help cause volcanoes. Some earthquakes can cause tsunamis. The type of earthquake most likely to cause a tsunami is one that causes the earth to move up and down versus an earthquake caused when two plates slide past each other, from north to south, for example. This kind of earthquake is more common near the coasts where one plate forces another plate down into the earth's interior.

DISASTER EFFECTS & HAZARDS FROM TSUNAMIS

You will have to prepare for and protect from primary disaster effects, including flooding, the destruction caused by impact from a solid wall of water, and very strong water currents. Some of the hazards that come with these effects include: destruction of bridges and buildings as the tsunami moves inland; people and objects, like cars, being carried inland then out to sea as the tsunami recedes; fires that start in fuel-soaked debris; and even radiation leaks from damaged nuclear power plants.

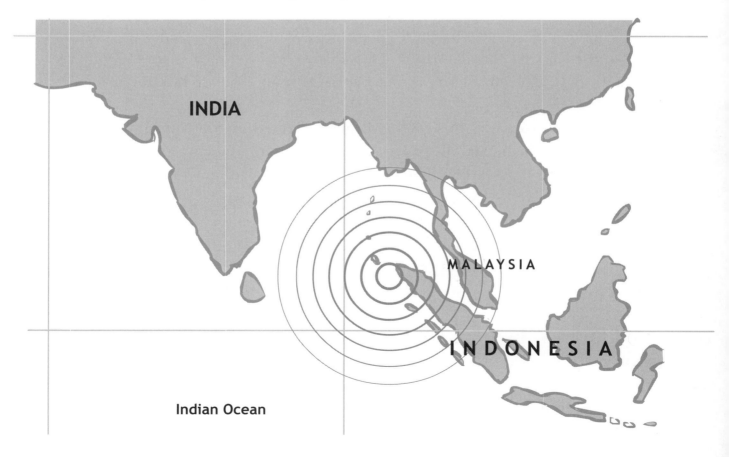

INDIA

MALAYSIA

INDONESIA

Indian Ocean

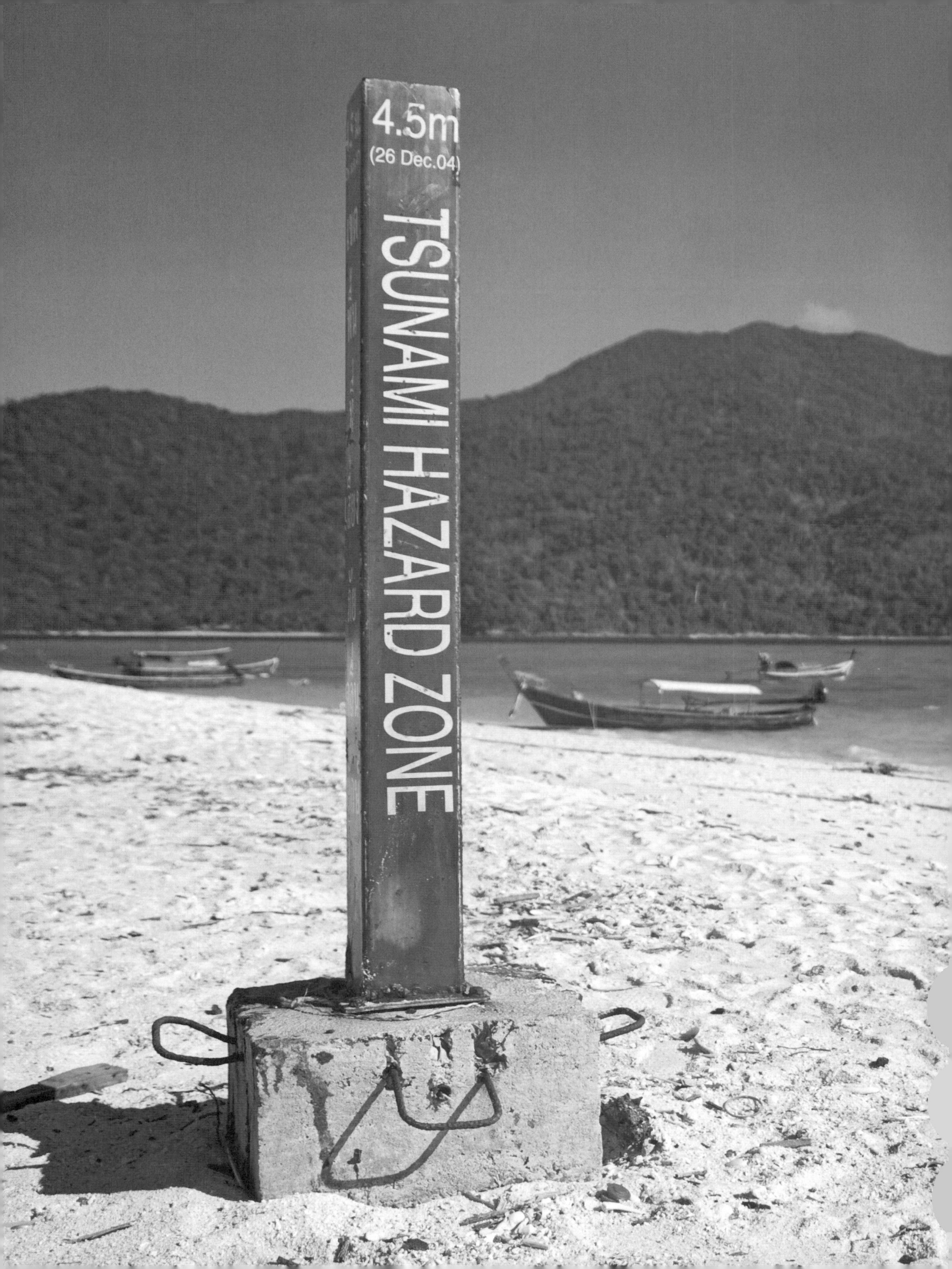
4.5m
(26 Dec.04)
TSUNAMI HAZARD ZONE

Travel times for tsunamis can be predicted with increasing accuracy. Hawaii and the West Coast of the U.S. had more than eight hours to get ready for the tsunami caused by the Great Eastern Japan Earthquake of 2011. Sendai, Japan, may have had as little as 15 minutes warning before the tsunami struck. Coastal populations located less than a few hundred miles from the location where a tsunami-generating event occurs are most vulnerable. They have very little time to react and try to escape the tsunami. Tsunami travel time is likely less than 30 minutes for many of these locations.

Tsunami Warning Centers (TWCs) are responsible for sending out alerts warning about the danger from a possible tsunami. The U.S. has two TWCs that cover alert responsibilities for the continental U.S., Alaska and Hawaii, as well as locations like Puerto Rico. The alert levels are described in the table below:

Tsunami Alert Levels:

Term	Description
Information Statement/Bulletin	An earthquake occurred and may generate a tsunami, or a tsunami advisory, watch or warning was issued for another section of the ocean that surrounds or borders your coast.
Advisory	Provides an advance alert to coastal populations about a tsunami watch or warning for other areas of the same ocean or that the tsunami poses no danger to their area.
Watch	Provides an advance alert to coastal populations that could be impacted by destructive tsunami waves. This is based on seismic information without the actual identification of a tsunami.
Warning	Provides an immediate alert to coastal populations that there is an imminent threat of a tsunami OR That a potentially destructive tsunami is on the way.

A key point is that even a tsunami warning may not stem from the sight of a tsunami. The TWCs monitor data and, based on the severity of the trigger event, like the size of an underwater earthquake, issue the appropriate alert.

PREPARE BEFORE TSUNAMIS

A potential or actual tsunami impacting the United States may come with very little warning. If the trigger event was a magnitude 9.0 earthquake 100 miles off the West Coast, some U.S. coastal population centers could have less than 15 minutes from the start of the earthquake to the arrival of the tsunami. If you live on the coast or are vacationing there, make sure you watch the news and Internet for any significant earthquake activity. Remem-

ber: earthquakes are a major trigger event for a tsunami. Plan your evacuation route to take you farther inland; where possible, follow higher ground and avoid bridges and other locations that are vulnerable to tsunami effects.

If anyone is in school, check with the school so you understand their policy regarding early release or cancellation of school due to major earthquake activity or if a tsunami advisory or watch is issued for the area. Make sure you sign up for any alert service the school has. Discuss who will pick up a child if the school closes early. What will the school do if there is a tsunami warning and, likely, no time to contact parents for early pick-up? Discuss this with any school-age children and help them understand how important it is to follow the teacher's instructions and get to higher ground or an upper floor in the school building as quickly and as safely as they can.

If you are vacationing on or near the shore of a large lake or inland sea, you could still be at risk from a tsunami. A major landslide or glacier calving into a large lake or inland sea could generate a tsunami. This could occur whether or not an earthquake actually triggered the landslide or glacier calving. Your best protections are information and mobility — the ability to evacuate quickly. Now, focus your preparations on your vehicle and your shelter-in-place location.

Maintain your vehicle — follow the guidance provided in Chapter 2. If you live on a coast or you vacation there, you must be prepared to evacuate immediately. Always keep at least half a tank of gas in your vehicle. Your ability to quickly evacuate away from the coast and move to higher ground is critical to your survival.

Update your emergency travel kit. Regardless of the time of year, make sure to pack thick socks and good walking shoes or boots for each person in your group. Refill your kit with water bottles, snack food and high-calorie food bars.

If you are vacationing on or near the coast, check with your hotel or lodging so you are aware of shelter-in-place and evacuation options should they be needed.

Maintain your shelter-in-place location — follow the guidance provided in Chapter 2. Be prepared to evacuate away from a tsunami much the same way you would from a volcano. If you live near the shoreline or you live in an area that is easily flooded by storm surge, your shelter is likely vulnerable to the effects of a tsunami. You might be able to use sand bags to shield your shelter from the rising floodwaters of a river, but this has no chance of success if you are in the direct path of a tsunami.

Update your emergency shelter-in-place kit. Regardless of the time of year, make sure to pack thick socks and good walking shoes or boots for each person in your group. This becomes even more important for those who will shelter away from their homes. If you live on high ground and your shelter is well suited to avoiding any primary disaster effects caused by a tsunami, consider stocking additional food and water. This will allow you to stay comfortably if a tsunami should damage roads and bridges, making short-term access to food, water and fuel a problem.

PROTECT FROM TSUNAMIS

A major earthquake has occurred offshore and a Tsunami Warning Center has issued a tsunami "Watch." Do you stay or do you evacuate?

To answer this, you need to know how far away you are from the coast and if you are on low-lying ground that would likely fill with water from the tsunami should it occur. According to the Federal Emergency Management Agency (FEMA), the primary danger area is within a mile of the shoreline or locations less than 25 feet above sea level. This does not mean that there is no danger if you are 2 miles from the shoreline, only that the "typical" tsunami will not be a direct threat to you and others. This is a "Watch," which means the danger level has increased significantly. If the alert had been a "Warning," it would mean there was an imminent threat from a tsunami or that a tsunami was already on the way.

Stay Informed

Follow news of the tsunami alert. How quickly can everyone gather if the group needs to evacuate? Watch for alerts from schools and daycare centers so you know if children will need to be picked up early. If you are within 1 mile of the coast or in a low-lying area near the coast, consider evacuating as quickly as you can.

If you wait until a "Warning" is declared or for a tsunami to occur, you may not have time to gather your family or group and evacuate safely. If you evacuate after the "Warning" is declared, you will likely become part of a crowd evacuation, reducing the speed at which you can leave the area as well as limiting your evacuation route options.

If you are on vacation near a coast, rely on sirens, alerts, the Internet and your contacts to let you know if there is a problem. Avoid the beach and nearshore locations if a tsunami "Watch" has been declared.

Be prepared for the "Watch" to become a Tsunami "Warning." If you live near a coast and you chose not to evacuate beforehand, you cannot wait to leave or spend much time to gather your group. Everyone who is at risk must evacuate now, from wherever they are located. Gather any children who are with you and try to evacuate inland or to nearby higher ground. Every minute you take to gather members of your group puts everyone who is already with the group at risk.

Take Action

A tsunami "Warning" has been announced for your area. A major earthquake may have just hit and there are still aftershocks, or the trigger event for the tsunami may not be as noticeable. The first sign of a tsunami could be warning sirens at the beach or the sudden flow of water out into the ocean, like watching the tide go out — but far too quickly. The onset of a tsunami could even include a loud roaring sound coming from the ocean. Regardless of which signs warn you of trouble, evacuate <u>immediately</u>.

Head to higher ground by moving away from the coast and, if possible, traveling up the steep slopes of hills. Stay away from shallow areas around a beach as these areas will provide the tsunami an easy path to travel inland. Any route that makes it easy for water to get to the ocean makes it easy for a tsunami to travel inland. This could be a drainage system, the mouth of a river or marshy lowlands, for example. Avoid these areas as you evacuate inland. Anyone separated from the group should evacuate on their own, following the same guidance to avoid tsunami effects.

If you do not have time or there is no nearby higher ground to travel to, go to a well-built multi-story building and climb up as many floors as you can. Stay inside the building and avoid any hallways that are open to the air and provide a direct path for water from the tsunami to pass through the building. If you have found a safe place to shelter from the tsunami, do not leave it until the tsunami has receded back into the ocean or body of water from which it came.

Check in with your long-distance contacts once you are safe. Let them know your status, which group members are with you and what injuries you may need medical help treating. You can also call local contacts farther from the coast if you think they were not affected by the tsunami or trigger event and ask for their help as needed.

You and your family or group can gather at your shelter-in-place location if it is far enough from the shoreline to be safe from the primary disaster effects of a tsunami. Follow the news and Internet, and listen for officials to declare that the danger from a tsunami is over and that the "Warning" has ended.

Communicate

When the tsunami is over, listen to the news and check the Internet. If you were forced to evacuate, can you return home or to where you were staying on vacation? If you sheltered in place, check your shelter for damage. If the tsunami was triggered by a large earthquake, make sure you follow the guidance in Chapter 8 and verify that your shelter is still safe to stay in.

A tsunami can do significant damage to an area, destroying bridges, and damaging or destroying buildings and roads. If the area was struck by an earthquake first, then the damage will be even greater. You may have to evacuate if too many essential services will not be restored before you would run out of food and water, or if there is a health hazard, like a radiation leak from a nearby nuclear power plant. If you do not have to evacuate, restock your shelter-in-place and emergency travel kits so you are prepared to respond should another disaster follow shortly after this one.

If you must evacuate, check with local and long-distance contacts and the authorities to identify the best route to leave the area. There could be major damage to roads and bridges as well as other hazards that could disrupt your evacuation from the area.

Whether you choose to stay or evacuate, let your local and long-distance contacts know your plans.

Seek medical evaluation and treatment for any injuries that occurred during the disaster.

YOUR CHECKLIST — TSUNAMIS

Prepare For Primary Disaster Effects — Tsunamis

❏ Update your emergency kits with additional supplies, including thick socks and good walking shoes or boots for each person in your group;

❏ Plan your evacuation route, even when just vacationing near the ocean;

❏ Make sure your vehicle always has at least half a tank of gas.

Protect From Primary Disaster Effects — Tsunamis

❏ Follow alerts; make sure children at schools and daycare are picked up;

❏ Evacuate if you are within a mile of the coast, or below 25 feet above sea level and near the coast:

    ❏ Best evacuation option: move inland and to higher ground;

    ❏ Good evacuation option: move to the upper floors of a strong multi-story building and shelter away from the direct path of the water from a tsunami;

    ❏ Call your long-distance contacts once you are safe and tell them you are evacuating and the route you are taking;

    ❏ Check the radio and Internet, and talk to your long-distance contacts before and as you evacuate so you can respond to any identified problems with your original evacuation route.

❏ If you shelter-in-place:

    ❏ Call your local and long-distance contacts and let them know your shelter location and that you are staying;

    ❏ Listen for local alerts and hazard warnings;

    ❏ Evacuate if your shelter location cannot protect you from these hazards;

    ❏ Talk regularly with your local and long-distance contacts. Let them know about any changes in your status, evaluate any new dangers they identify, and decide whether to stay or evacuate based on the new information.

For actions after the disaster, see page 57.

Notes

Notes

Notes

Chapter 11:
Outbreaks & Epidemics

SCAN FOR CHAPTER
OVERVIEW VIDEO

Some disasters begin with a simple cough or runny nose. Disease outbreaks have occurred from ancient times to the present. An outbreak or an epidemic, which is a disease outbreak that has spread over a broad area, can cause widespread sickness and even death. The worst of these outbreaks can kill people of all ages because few people have an acquired immunity to the disease. However, your preparations and response to an outbreak or epidemic will help you reduce the chance of serious illness and death.

WHY SHOULD YOU BE CONCERNED?

Disease outbreaks are a part of our world. They are not limited to a location or time of year. Heat and humidity make it easier for the spread of some diseases, like those that can be carried by mosquitoes and other insects. In general, your body resists diseases based on what it has fought previously. When people are exposed to a new disease that their body does not recognize, it can be much harder for the body to fight off the disease. In severe cases, the disease can actually kill hundreds of thousands of people or more before the bodies of survivors have learned to fight off the new disease.

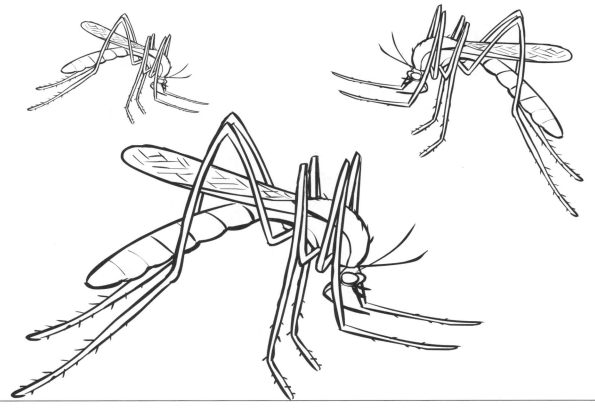

In an average year, about 30,000 Americans die from the flu, making it a deadly killer. This loss of life is tragic but it pales beside one disease-related disaster from our past. The Influenza Pandemic of 1918 — also called the 1918 Spanish Flu — killed 675,000 Americans and 40 to 60 million people globally. It was thought to have infected 25 percent of the U.S. population and some 500 million people globally. According to the Centers for Disease Control and Prevention (CDC), this flu originated in Asia and was a new version of the avian flu. People had little or no immunity to this dangerous mutation of the avian flu, and it killed those in prime health as well as the very young and elderly.

What Causes Outbreaks & Epidemics?

Disease outbreaks and epidemics have a variety of causes, including: the spread of a new strain of disease; migration of disease-bearing insects, animals and birds into new areas; breakdown of healthcare and sanitation after other disasters; as well as malnutrition and failure to properly vaccinate against known diseases.

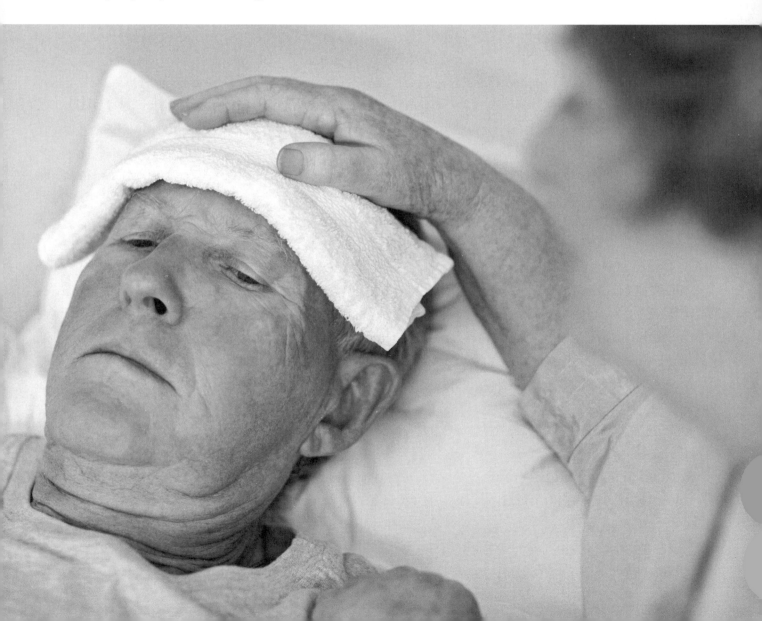

In some cases, the authorities can predict the increased occurrence of a particular disease because they understand how it is spread. In the U.S., there is an increasing problem with the West Nile Virus, which is spread by infected mosquitoes. As the climate warms up, these mosquitoes are able to survive and spread farther north than they could have in the past. People with limited or no immunity are now being exposed to this disease, resulting in an increase in illness, as well as some deaths.

DISASTER EFFECTS & HAZARDS

You will have to prepare for and protect from disease outbreaks and epidemics. Epidemics can be widespread. If the epidemic is deadly and easily spread by human contact, like the 1918 Spanish Flu, then you could see the disruption of many services you rely on. These secondary disaster effects could include the loss of many essential, very important and important services discussed in Chapter 3.

The authorities can limit basic freedoms that are taken for granted if they feel these limits are necessary to protect the public's safety. Some examples of these limitations include travel, routine medical services access and freedom to gather in public. Travel restrictions could impact your ability to evacuate or return home if you are on vacation when an epidemic strikes. Medical services could be limited if hospitals and doctor's offices are overwhelmed caring for the infected. Schools, places of worship, sports facilities and malls, for example, could be closed to prevent people from gathering in enclosed spaces and more easily spreading the disease.

Many people could decide to limit contact with other people by working from home or not going to work and calling in sick. Any business that is heavily reliant on large numbers of people to function could suffer, operating for fewer hours in a given week, fewer locations or even closing due to a lack of staff, let alone customers.

There is no way to predict when the next dangerous epidemic will strike. Since the year 2000, there has already been one declared global pandemic, due to the H1N1 strain of influenza A, also known as the Swine Flu. Thankfully, this disease outbreak did not have the lethal effects that the 1918 Spanish Flu did. Your actions to prepare for and protect from disease outbreaks and epidemics can improve your ability to avoid infection and, if infected, limit its spread among your family or group and beyond.

PREPARE BEFORE OUTBREAKS & EPIDEMICS

Some of the services you rely on — like food access, fuel delivery and drug prescriptions as needed — could be limited or severely disrupted for weeks or longer, depending on the severity of the epidemic, how long it takes to develop the vaccine and vaccinate the U.S. population, and how long the disease continues to spread and infect others.

There will always be a small portion of the population that cannot be vaccinated for certain diseases. This may be due to allergies, for example, or the vaccination may be unhealthy for pregnant women. This group can be partially protected by what is called Herd Immunity. This means that a small part of a population has some protection when a disease cannot easily spread to them because so many other people are resistant to it.

Herd Immunity can help protect family members and friends who cannot be vaccinated or have weakened immune systems. Herd Immunity only has a chance to work when there is a very high rate of vaccination or immunity among the rest of the population. Talk with your family or group about the importance of being up to date with all vaccinations; those who can get vaccinated should. This is a way to help your body build up its defenses against known diseases. Get the annual flu shot, because it can help protect you against the most likely strains of flu the authorities believe you will face in a given year.

There are everyday actions you can take to better avoid or limit the effects of a disease outbreak or epidemic. You may already be practicing some of these good health habits, but please read on to see if there are any other practices below that might help you and others:

- Ensure every person has their own toothbrush and toothpaste to avoid passing germs from mouth to mouth. Do not share a drinking glass;
- Cover your mouth or nose with a tissue or your arm when you sneeze. If you use your hand, you can easily pass germs from person to person;
- Wash your hands with soap and water or use hand sanitizer, especially after you cough or sneeze;
- Avoid touching your eyes, nose or mouth to avoid spreading germs;
- Stay at home if you are sick. Do not return to work or go out in public until you are free from both a fever and its effects for at least 24 hours;
- While sick, limit contact with others to avoid spreading the infection.

Maintain your vehicle by following the guidance provided in Chapter 2. Plan several evacuation routes to ensure you are not trapped if another disaster strikes while you are responding to the effects of an epidemic. The authorities could restrict travel to limit the spread of the disease. Even if you cannot evacuate, you will still need your vehicle in the event an emergency puts you on the road. Keep your vehicle fueled at half a tank or more.

Update your emergency travel kit. Store it in your vehicle and keep it fully stocked with medicine as well as food and water for you and your pets. Make sure to pack seasonal clothing as well as thick socks and good walking shoes or boots for each person in your group. Pack a portable solar charger and water-purification device, just in case your trip takes longer than expected or you have to leave your vehicle. Buy facemasks, like surgical masks, or N95 respirators, which are a kind of mask used in construction to avoid breathing in dust and other small particles. These may be able to help protect from airborne germs.

Maintain your shelter-in-place location by following the guidance provided in Chapter 2. Plan ahead in case someone in your family or group gets sick and needs to be isolated

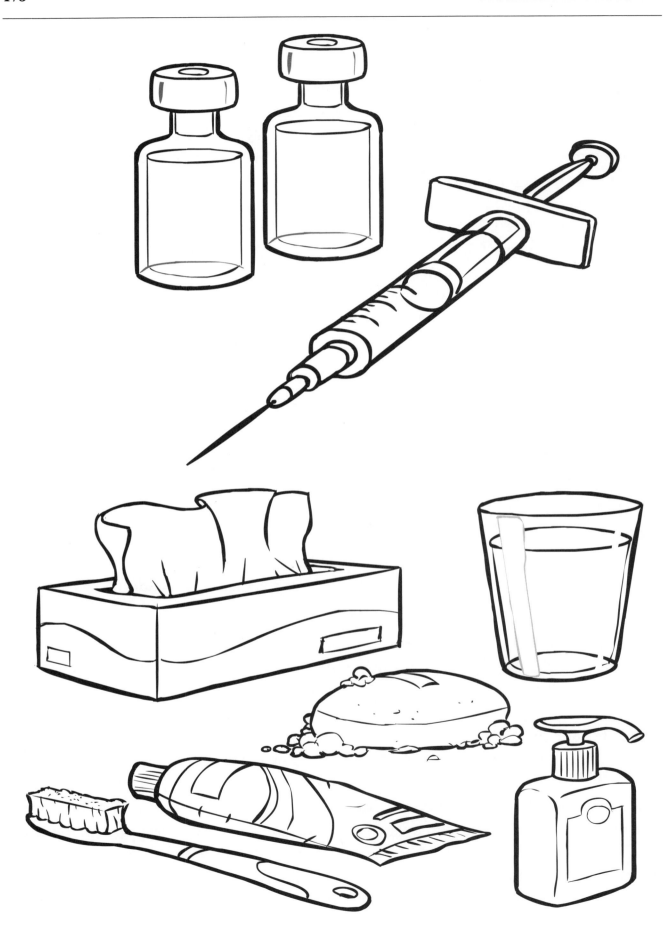

from everyone else. You will need a separate room with at least one bed. If there is a connected bathroom or a bathroom that can be set aside for the sick, that is even better.

Update your emergency shelter-in-place kit. Pack seasonal clothing as well as thick socks and good walking shoes or boots for each person in your group. Stock up on food and water for you and your pets, as well as fuel, like propane, to cook your food. Add in extra medicine, including prescriptions or the best non-prescription substitutes your pharmacist can identify. Make sure you have a portable water filter and a portable solar charger in case you lose water pressure or power. Buy facemasks or N95 respirators to help protect from airborne germs.

Your goal is to be self-sufficient for at least two weeks. You may choose to stock up with enough supplies to last longer than this if you believe that the outbreak or epidemic could last beyond two weeks.

Protect From Outbreaks & Epidemics

Perhaps there is an early warning about a new disease spreading across the U.S. or there is a major increase in the number of adults and children in your area who are out sick. In either case, you become concerned that a disease outbreak or worse, an epidemic, is happening. What do you do?

Stay Informed

Follow news about any warnings. The director of Health and Human Services (HHS) can declare a health emergency because of the presence of an infectious disease that could become an epidemic. If there is no specific news but you are concerned, check with your doctor's office or county health officials. They may have information they can share with you or put your mind at ease about what they believe may be a bad, but normal, flu season. You can also check the CDC website for information on disease and other alerts at: http://emergency.cdc.gov/recentincidents.asp.

Talk with your family or group to share information about whether or not anyone is sick and likely contagious. If anyone is contagious, they should be isolated in a different room. Once you believe you are facing a disease outbreak or epidemic, you need to act.

If you are traveling and you hear about an outbreak or epidemic along your travel route or at your destination, change your plans unless it is an emergency. If it is an emergency, you will have to take extra precautions to try to avoid getting exposed or infected.

Take Action

Contact your doctor's office, tell them the symptoms of anyone who is sick and follow their guidance. Gather your family or group and put anyone who is sick in a different room, preferably with an attached bathroom, or, where possible, give them a separate bathroom solely for their use. This could be a bad case of the seasonal flu or something worse. The best case is that those who are sick are asked to come to the doctor's office where they are diagnosed, given a vaccine and allowed to rest at home — isolated from others until they are no longer contagious.

If there is a bad epidemic, there may be no vaccine when the first members of your family or group get sick. The doctor's office may be able to help or might be limited to calling in several prescriptions for the sick, treating symptoms like fever while the authorities work to create a vaccine. It is possible that the hospitals and doctor's offices will be overwhelmed trying to care for those with life-threatening injuries as well as those infected by the epidemic. Follow the instructions of the medical experts and authorities. Be prepared to take care of sick family or group members without a lot of help from doctors or emergency services personnel. Each family or group should discuss and decide which person will care for the sick. This is the only person who should go in and out of the room set aside for the sick, bringing them food and water and taking care of their needs.

This caregiver will be at greater risk than the remaining healthy members of the group. This person must be very careful not to spread germs when entering or leaving the sick room. He or she will benefit most from wearing a mask from the survival kit. These masks do not replace the good health habits discussed earlier. Instead, they can help keep your chosen caregiver healthy. Keep up other healthy habits such as getting enough sleep, drinking plenty of fluids and eating well-balanced meals, because this will benefit everyone in your family or group. If the temperature is not too hot or cold, consider closing the vents in the sick room to limit the spread of airborne germs.

Periodically check the Internet, radio and TV to get updates on the disaster. Once a vaccine is available, follow instructions on how to get it. It is possible that the authorities will rely on the U.S. Postal Service to deliver vaccines in some areas. Be patient and follow the instructions provided via TV and the Internet. If the epidemic is caused by a new virus that no one has had before, everyone will need the vaccine, and it will take time to create and distribute the vaccine to the entire U.S. population.

Keep in touch with your local and long-distance contacts to let them know your status. If you have any life-threatening injuries, they may be able to help you find medical assistance even if there are problems getting into the doctor's offices and hospitals in your area.

Communicate

Have you and your family or group been vaccinated? Have the authorities stopped all the emergency measures they took to limit the spread of the disease in your area? Listen to the TV and follow the Internet and radio. If the emergency measures end, then the disease outbreak or epidemic should be over soon. The risk of getting infected is still real, but now that you are vaccinated, you are back to facing diseases that you should have some ability to resist.

Check your shelter for damage and make sure it is still safe for continued use. Restock your shelter-in-place and emergency travel kits so you are prepared to respond should another disaster follow shortly after this one.

Seek medical evaluation and treatment for any injuries that occurred during the disaster.

YOUR CHECKLIST —
OUTBREAKS & EPIDEMICS

Prepare For Primary Disaster Effects — Outbreaks & Epidemics:

❑ Practice good health habits:
- ❑ Don't share your toothbrush, toothpaste, or drinking glass;
- ❑ Cover your mouth or nose with a tissue or your arm when you sneeze;
- ❑ Wash your hands with soap and water or use hand sanitizer, especially after you cough or sneeze;
- ❑ Avoid touching your eyes, nose or mouth to avoid spreading germs;
- ❑ Stay at home if you are sick; do not return to work or go out in public until you are free from both a fever and its effects for at least 24 hours;
- ❑ While sick, limit contact with others to avoid spreading the infection;

❑ Update your emergency kits with additional supplies, including: thick socks and good walking shoes or boots for each person in your group; a portable water purification device and solar charger; and facemasks or N95 respirators;

❑ Update your shelter kit with at least two weeks of food and water for your family or group, including any pets;

❑ Plan multiple evacuation routes in case one becomes unsafe;

❑ Make sure your vehicle always has at least half a tank of gas.

Protect From Primary Disaster Effects — Outbreaks & Epidemics

❑ Follow news about any warnings; if there is no specific news but you are concerned, check with your doctor's office or county health officials;

❑ Contact your doctor's office, tell them the symptoms of anyone who is sick and follow their guidance; if the sick cannot stay at the hospital, care for them at home;

❑ Isolate anyone who is sick in a different room, with an attached bathroom or a bathroom set aside just for those who are sick;

❑ Treat with a vaccine, if it is available; treat symptoms like a fever;

❑ Choose one person to care for the sick; this person wears a facemask or N95 respirator when taking care of the sick;

❑ Keep up other healthy habits like getting enough sleep, drinking plenty of fluids, and eating well-balanced meals;

❑ Close the vents in the sick room if temperatures allow;

❑ Avoid large gatherings to limit the spread of the disease;

❑ Once a vaccine is available, follow instructions on how to get it;

❏ Check the radio and Internet, and talk to your long-distance contacts so you know when any restrictions have been lifted and you can resume normal activities;

❏ Check with your doctor's office and the local hospital so you know when you can bring in anyone who has lingering injuries;

❏ Keep your local and long-distance contacts informed about your status and use their assistance as needed.

For actions after the disaster, see page 57.

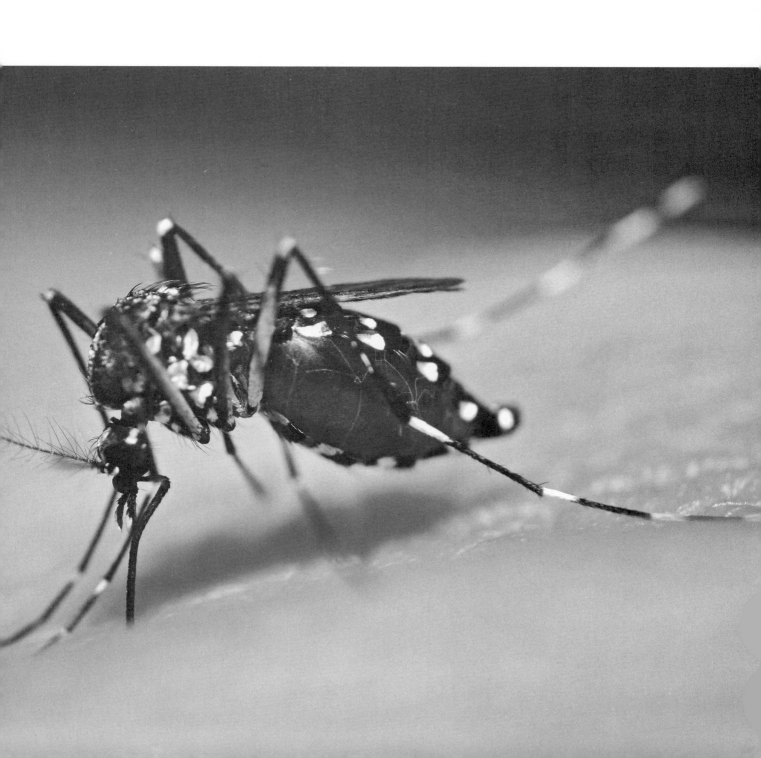

Notes

Notes

Notes

Chapter 12:
Industrial Disasters

SCAN FOR CHAPTER OVERVIEW VIDEO

In previous chapters, you learned about a variety of natural disasters as well as the primary and secondary disaster effects you may have to overcome. Chapter 12, Industrial Disasters, is the first of two chapters that talk about the broader category of man-caused disasters.

An industrial disaster can be caused by the failure of man-made equipment — which can vary from a tanker truck to a nuclear power plant — resulting in a disaster. Whether the failure of the equipment was due to damage from another disaster or poor construction does not matter. What matters is how you respond to the effects of the disaster to protect yourself and your family or group.

WHY SHOULD YOU BE CONCERNED?

Industrial disasters can and will happen. They are not limited to a particular region or coast. They are, however, more likely to happen in an area where there are significant industrial activities. If you live in an area near a refinery, a chemical plant or power plant, you are more likely to experience an industrial accident than if you lived in a rural area far from this level of industry. Regardless of where you live, though, you can be impacted by the effects of an industrial disaster. Roads and railways can take potentially dangerous substances, like toxic chemicals or gasoline, through locations that have little if any nearby industrial activity. A derailed train or tanker truck accident can release these hazards near you.

One of the worst industrial disasters in history occurred in December 1984 when toxic gas leaked from a Union Carbide plant in Bhopal, India. The leak occurred at night and affected a densely populated area nearby, spreading out to kill thousands of people. It also injured more than 500,000 people, according to an Indian government affidavit released in 2006.

In March 2011, the Great Eastern Japan Earthquake created a tsunami that badly damaged the Fukushima Daiichi nuclear power plant and the grid that provided primary power to its systems. The cooling systems lost power and three of the reactors at the site suffered at least a partial meltdown, releasing radiation into the seawater and air.

Some disasters happen when our growing reliance on technology collides with natural cycles that have been occurring since before recorded history. One of these natural cycles is related to solar storm activity. Scientists have identified an 11-year sunspot cycle, reflecting a natural increase and decrease in the occurrence of sunspots. They can cause solar storms that leave the sun and spread out into our solar system, with the potential to affect you here on Earth. These storms not only cause the Northern Lights, but they can damage satellites and sensitive electronic devices, as well as overload power lines, causing widespread power outages. Scientists believe that a very bad solar storm could cause widespread damage to the power grid and power outages that could last a month or more before power was restored to certain areas.

WHAT CAUSES INDUSTRIAL DISASTERS?

Industrial disasters can be caused by other disasters, like an earthquake or wildfire; by natural cycles, like the sunspot cycle that can create a bad solar storm; or even by failure of a safety device that would normally have prevented the disaster from occurring.

Modern society relies on the use of electronic devices in almost every aspect of daily life. These devices include cell phones, computers, medical equipment, and even the ignition switches in most vehicles. They are designed to work in spite of the minor power changes that occur in the power grid as part of normal power generation and distribution. These devices are not designed to work when they are affected by large power shifts and electrical currents that can occur in the most severe solar storms; they can be disabled, damaged or even destroyed by the effects of these storms.

DISASTER EFFECTS & HAZARDS

You will have to prepare for and protect from a variety of primary disaster effects, depending on the kind of industrial disaster that occurs. As you learned in earlier chapters, some of these effects are mobile, like fire, toxic gas and radiation, and can limit your ability to shelter-in-place. Hazards will also be related to the kind of industrial disaster that occurs.

Severe space weather events, like a geomagnetic storm or strong solar flare, can create a disaster here on Earth. In March 1989, a magnetic storm caused the collapse of the Hydro-Quebec grid in Canada. This resulted in a nine-hour power outage across much of the province of Quebec, impacting some 6 million people. This same storm caused several hundred other events across North America, including the failure of a nuclear power plant transformer on the East Coast.

In the last 200 years, the most severe space weather event to affect Earth occurred during August and September 1859. This geomagnetic storm, called the Carrington Event, had effects that were evident across North America and Europe. During the worst part of this storm, people in the Northeast could read newspapers at night using the Northern Lights as their only light source. Telegraph operators in the U.S. and Europe disconnected their batteries, relying on the electricity the storm imparted to their lines to continue working. Some electricity surges were bad enough to burn telegraph operators and start fires.

In 2008, the National Academy of Sciences published a report warning about the dangers the U.S. would face if this storm occurred now. Some of the effects of a solar storm this severe would include the interruption of radio and other forms of communication, failure of many electronic systems, like transportation and modern medical equipment, as well as potentially long-term damage to the power grid that could take months or longer to fix.

Solar storms are real and they do vary in strength, as history has shown. Just as certain conditions in the ocean help create the chance for more dangerous hurricanes, there are conditions on the sun that help create stronger solar storms. While scientists may not fully understand these conditions, you must still prepare for and protect from the storms that they can cause.

PREPARE BEFORE AN INDUSTRIAL DISASTER

Industrial disasters can involve stationary effects, like a building damaged by an explosion, as well as mobile effects, like a fire or toxic gas leak. Start your preparations by learning about the dangers around you. Do you have an industrial plant or complex within 10 miles

of where you live? Does it use, produce or store a significant amount of a dangerous substance, like gasoline or a toxic gas? If you are not sure, contact local authorities and ask about any industrial hazards you should prepare for.

Roads and railroads can create a danger for you if a vehicle carrying a hazardous substance has an accident releasing that substance. This is more difficult to prepare for since you do not know the specific hazard you could face. Focus on what you know from prior chapters. If the effect is mobile, you are more likely to evacuate away from the effect. If the effect is stationary, than you can usually shelter-in-place, unless your shelter is damaged and unsafe to stay in.

You know you will face solar storms in the future, but you don't know when one will have the power to really affect you. It is the responsibility of the authorities and companies involved in power generation and distribution to protect those systems from the effects of a very dangerous solar storm. If this storm comes, it will impact you.

A solar storm like the one that hit the U.S. and Europe in 1859 will impact our electronic infrastructure, what we rely on for day-to-day living. There will be problems with communications, computers and electrical systems, but we don't know how bad those problems will be. You could lose power for a week or longer; face problems with transportation; and have access to limited or no medical services for an extended period of time. You already know how to prepare for these conditions from what was discussed in prior chapters. This particular disaster means that you may have to do without many essential, very important and important services for a longer period of time, so plan for this with your family or group.

Maintain your vehicle. Follow the guidance provided in Chapter 2. Plan several evacuation routes to ensure you are not trapped if an industrial disaster cuts off one route. Keep your vehicle fueled at half a tank or more. Keep your emergency travel kit fully stocked and in your vehicle.

Update your emergency travel kit. Store it in your vehicle and keep it fully stocked with medicine as well as food and water for you and your pets. Make sure to pack seasonal clothing as well as thick socks and good walking shoes or boots for each person in your group. Pack a portable solar charger and water-purification device, just in case your trip takes longer than expected or you have to leave your vehicle.

Maintain your shelter-in-place location. Follow the guidance provided in Chapter 2. You may have to shelter-in-place because of a toxic gas release you cannot evacuate away from. Add plastic sheeting and duct tape to your kit so you can seal your shelter-in-place location. Heavy plastic trash bags will work if plastic sheeting is not available.

Update your emergency shelter-in-place kit. Pack seasonal clothing as well as thick socks and good walking shoes or boots for each person in your group. Stock up on food and water for you and your pets as well as fuel, like propane, to cook your food. Add extra medicine, including prescriptions or the best non-prescription substitutes your pharmacist can identify. Make sure you have a portable water filter so you can restock your water supply using rain water or untreated water should you lose water pressure. Include a portable solar charger to charge cell and satellite phones in case your power is out but cell phone towers and satellites are still working. If you have bikes, store several in or near your shelter location for use after the disaster.

Your goal is to be self-sufficient for at least a week. You may choose to stock up with enough supplies to last weeks or more if you think the authorities are not likely to be able to help after one week's time. The choice is yours. You and your family or group are the ones who will benefit most from the preparations you make now, before a disaster comes.

Protect From Industrial Disasters

The authorities have issued an alert about toxic chemicals spreading downwind from a major industrial accident or they have issued a warning about a severe solar storm that will hit Earth in the next 24 hours. What do you do?

Stay Informed

Follow news of the accident or solar storm warning. How much time do you and others have to react? Are the primary disaster effects mobile, like a gas cloud or fire, or stationary, like damage to a power plant or bridge? Watch for alerts from schools and daycare centers so you know if children will need to be picked up early. Listen to the authorities for updates on the dangers you will face and the actions you should take to protect yourself and others.

If you are traveling when you hear about an accident or solar storm warning, call your long-distance contacts and ask them to help you stay informed. Act on warnings from the authorities as well as the information your long-distance contacts can provide.

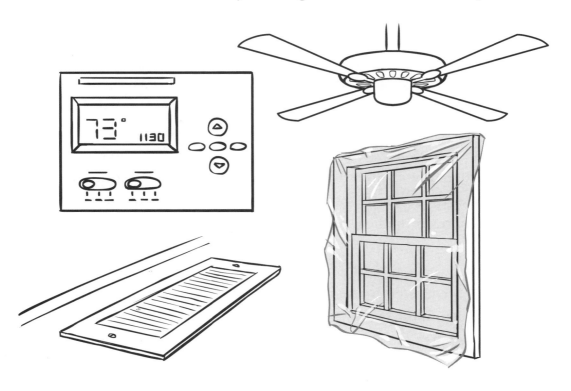

Take Action

You are in danger from an industrial accident or coming solar storm. Your first warning may be the sound of sirens, an Internet alert or an emergency broadcast on the radio or TV. If the disaster effects are mobile and threaten your shelter location, like a fire, you must evacuate. Decide whether or not you have time to gather your family or group and evacuate together. Pick up children from schools and daycare centers. If you cannot evacuate together, everyone should call your long-distance contacts. They can coordinate a safe place along the evacuation route where everyone can meet.

If you are in danger from a toxic gas cloud, evacuation is the best option. If you do not have time to evacuate, you need to stop airflow into your shelter location. Turn off your heating or air conditioning and any fans; close and lock doors; close any vents, including any fireplace dampers. Gather all the people and pets in your family or group into the room you will seal. Consider using a bedroom with a connected bathroom for personal hygiene. Make sure your shelter-in-place kit and emergency radio are with you. Seal all windows, vents and doors to the room using the plastic sheeting and duct tape in your shelter-in-place kit.

You may have to rely on schools or daycare centers to shelter children at their locations. Call any children separated from the group and not in school. If you have no time to evacuate, it may not be safe for them to try to return home. If they cannot return home before the danger arrives, they should shelter where they are or move away from the disaster area, based on whether or not they are in immediate danger.

Periodically check the Internet, radio and TV to get updates on the disaster. Do not unseal your room until the authorities have declared that there is no more danger from the toxic gas cloud.

If you are in danger from a severe solar storm, listen for instructions from the authorities. Gather your family or group to shelter-in-place. Remember, you do not know how bad the solar storm will be or what services will be affected. Take action as though you expect to lose power and communications for at least a few days. If this does not happen, that is great! If it does, you prepared for it and now you act on your plans. Follow the instructions in Chapter 3 on actions to take if you lose power for three to seven days.

Whether you evacuated or sheltered-in-place, check in with your long-distance contacts once you are safe. Let them know your status, which group members are with you, and what injuries you may need medical help treating.

Communicate

When the disaster is over, listen to the news and check the Internet. If you were forced to evacuate, can you return home or to where you were staying on vacation? If you sheltered-in-place, check your shelter for damage to make sure it is safe for continued use.

You may have to evacuate if too many essential services will not be restored before you would run out of food and water or if there is a health hazard, like a radiation leak from a nearby nuclear power plant. If you do not have to evacuate, restock your shelter-in-place and emergency travel kits so you are prepared to respond should another disaster follow shortly after this one.

Seek medical evaluation and treatment for any injuries that occurred during the disaster.

YOUR CHECKLIST — INDUSTRIAL DISASTERS

Prepare For Primary Disaster Effects — Industrial Disasters

❑ Update your emergency kits with additional supplies, including: thick socks and good walking shoes or boots for each person in your group; a portable water-purification device; and solar charger;

❑ Update your emergency shelter-in-place kit with plastic sheeting and duct tape. Consider cutting it to size for the room you will seal;

❑ Plan multiple evacuation routes in case one becomes unsafe;

❑ Make sure your vehicle always has at least half a tank of gas.

Protect From Primary Disaster Effects — Industrial Disasters

❑ Follow alerts. Pick up children at schools and daycare if you have enough warning time, otherwise, children shelter at their locations;

❑ Evacuate from mobile effects like fire or a toxic gas cloud;
   Check the radio and Internet, and talk to your long-distance contacts before and as you evacuate so you can respond to any identified problems with your original evacuation route;

❑ Shelter-in-place from stationary effects or if you cannot evacuate ahead of the disaster effect's arrival:
   ❑ Close and lock doors, close all vents and fireplace dampers;
   ❑ Seal your shelter location if there is a toxic gas hazard;
   ❑ Children who cannot return home safely should shelter where they are or move away from mobile effects;
   ❑ Check the radio and Internet, and talk to your long-distance contacts to make sure it is safe before you unseal your shelter location;

❑ If you shelter-in-place from a severe solar storm:
   ❑ Store several bikes in or near your shelter location for use after the disaster;
   ❑ Consider adding enough food and water to your emergency shelter-in-place kit to sustain you, your family or group, and pets for at least seven days;
   ❑ Store additional water in spare containers for both drinking and personal hygiene;

❑ Listen for local alerts and hazard warnings. Evacuate if your shelter location cannot protect you from these hazards;

❑ Talk regularly with your local and long-distance contacts. Let them know about any changes in your status, evaluate any new dangers they identify, and decide whether to stay or evacuate based on the new information.

For actions after the disaster, see page 57.

Notes

Notes

Notes

Chapter 13:
Terrorist Disasters

SCAN FOR CHAPTER OVERVIEW VIDEO

Terrorism has many definitions linked by a common thread — the use of violence against others. The key for this chapter is not the definition, but rather, that terrorists will use a variety of methods, including explosives, aircraft and poisonous gas, to try to kill people and damage or destroy infrastructure like buildings, bridges and nuclear power plants.

Chapter 13, Terrorist Disasters, is the second chapter in the broader category of man-caused disasters. Some acts of terrorism, like the attack on the World Trade Center, may cause a disaster. You cannot predict when an act of terrorism will occur or what the resulting disaster will be. You can, however, prepare for and protect from disasters caused by terrorist acts.

WHY SHOULD YOU BE CONCERNED?

Terrorist acts will occur, and some of these acts will cause a disaster that could affect you. If, for example, you live near or work in high-profile government or corporate facilities, there is a greater likelihood you will have to react to a terrorist attack and the potential disaster that follows it. Like industrial disasters, terrorist disasters will not be limited to a particular region or coast. Man-caused disasters can occur in rural areas using the local road and rail network. Disasters in these areas could begin with terrorists intentionally derailing a train or causing a tanker truck accident.

It is harder to prepare for a particular disaster since the terrorists will choose when and what to attack and what kind of disaster they will try to create. Don't focus on the unknowns regarding the disaster terrorists can create; instead, focus on what you know you can do — prepare for and protect from different kinds of disasters. Throughout this book, you have learned how to prepare for and protect from a wide variety of disasters. Regardless of what the disaster is or how it happens, you know you have a better chance to avoid injury or worse when you prepare before any disaster occurs.

WHAT CAUSES TERRORIST DISASTERS?

Terrorist disasters are caused by the intentional acts of one or more individuals with the goal to injure or kill people as well as damage or destroy infrastructure, like power plants, bridges and hospitals. These acts to harm or destroy can include the use of fire, poisonous gas, explosives, highly flammable substances like gasoline, radioactive materials and even biological agents, like anthrax.

Disaster Effects & Hazards

Disaster effects and the resulting hazards from acts of terrorism can be similar to many of the effects and hazards you could face from an industrial disaster. You will have to prepare for and protect from a wide variety of primary disaster effects. These include effects that are mobile, like fire and toxic gas; effects that are stationary, like damage to a bridge or power plant; and effects that can be spread from contact, like a biological agent that causes a dangerous disease to infect most of the people who come in contact with it.

The Department of Homeland Security (DHS) was created in response to the terrorist attacks against the United States on Sept. 11, 2001. It has the responsibility to prepare for, protect from, respond to, and help recover from natural and man-made disasters, including terrorism. The DHS implemented the National Terrorism Advisory System (NTAS) in April 2011 to replace the Homeland Security Alert System (HSAS). The HSAS was the prior system that identified the risk of terrorist attack using a scale of colors ranging from green, low risk of attack, up to red, severe risk of attack. The new system was implemented to provide more detailed information about specific threats; to communicate this information to those who need it most; and to tell you and others what actions you can take in response to a possible terrorist attack.

The NTAS has two alert levels: Elevated Threat Alert, which warns of a credible terrorist threat against the United States; and Imminent Threat Alert, which warns of a credible, specific and impending terrorist threat against the United States (Source: www.dhs.gov/files/programs/ntas.shtm).

Alerts can be given an expiration date and they can also be updated to reflect new information. Consider signing up for the NTAS email alert system or, if you prefer, sign up for alerts via social media like Facebook and Twitter. If you want to sign up for one or more of these services, enter the web address above using the Internet and follow the instructions provided.

Prepare Before Terrorist Disasters

You have control over how you prepare for and protect from disasters, regardless of how they happen. Your vigilance, watching your surroundings and letting the authorities know if something suspicious is going on, can help protect you and others from acts of terrorism and the disasters that could follow.

"If You See Something, Say Something™" is a public-awareness campaign started by DHS in 2010. One part of preparing for a disaster caused by a terrorist act is to help stop it before it happens. Your vigilance can help reduce the likelihood of a man-caused disaster. If a worker at a chemical plant catches a maintenance error and fixes it, an industrial disaster might have been prevented. In the same way, if you see something suspicious, call 911 and tell the authorities. It might be nothing but it could also be everything to the people who get to live because you took action.

The vigilance of you and others will not prevent every act of terrorism or the disasters that may be caused by these acts. You will still need to prepare for the effects of the disasters you could face. These effects fall into three general categories: mobile effects, stationary effects, and effects that can be spread from contact. Focus on how you would prepare and protect from these types of effects.

As you learned in Chapter 12, some man-caused disasters produce effects that are mobile. If you are facing an effect that moves, be prepared to move away from it, just like you would move away from a fire.

If you are facing a stationary effect, you can probably stay in your shelter-in-place location. Before you make the decision to stay or go, you need to understand this stationary effect. Is it a bridge you can no longer use for an evacuation route or is it a nuclear power plant that has been so badly damaged that it may start leaking radiation? If a stationary effect is likely to cause other primary disaster effects that will pose a danger to you, then you should evacuate.

The last effect category is usually associated with a major disease outbreak or epidemic. If you are warned about a major outbreak of a dangerous disease that spreads easily from person to person, then you are probably safer staying in your shelter location. You need to limit the amount of contact you have with people outside your family or group to reduce the chance of catching the disease.

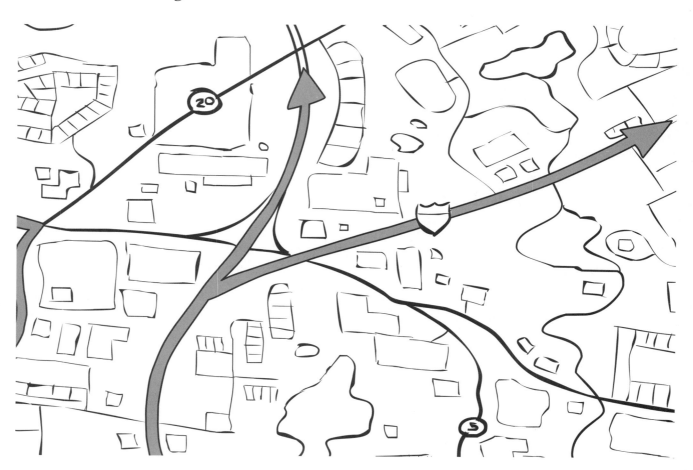

Regardless of the disaster effect you are trying to prepare for and protect from, you will rely on information, mobility and a well-prepared shelter-in-place to reduce the chance of injury or worse. Most of your preparations are the same as if you were preparing for an unknown industrial disaster.

Maintain your vehicle. Follow the guidance provided in Chapter 2. Plan several evacuation routes to ensure you are not trapped if a terrorist-caused disaster cuts off one route. Keep your vehicle fueled at half a tank or more.

Update your emergency travel kit. Store it in your vehicle and keep it fully stocked with medicine as well as food and water for you and your pets. Make sure to pack seasonal clothing as well as thick socks and good walking shoes or boots for each person in your group. Pack a portable solar charger and water-purification device, just in case your trip takes longer than expected or you have to leave your vehicle.

Maintain your shelter-in-place location. Follow the guidance provided in Chapter 2. You may have to shelter-in-place because of a toxic gas release you cannot evacuate away from. Add plastic sheeting and duct tape to your kit so that you can seal your shelter-in-place location. Heavy plastic trash bags will work if plastic sheeting is not available.

Update your emergency shelter-in-place kit. Pack seasonal clothing as well as thick socks and good walking shoes or boots for each person in your group. Stock up on food and water for you and your pets, as well as fuel, like propane, to cook your food. Add in extra

medicine, including prescriptions or the best non-prescription substitutes your pharmacist can identify. Make sure you have a portable water-purification device so you can restock your water supply using rain water or untreated water should you lose water pressure. Include a portable solar charger to charge cell and satellite phones in case your power is out but cell phone towers and satellites are still working. If you have bikes, store several in or near your shelter location for use after the disaster.

Your goal is to be self-sufficient for at least three to seven days. If the U.S. is facing a widespread disease outbreak, what is often called an epidemic, the authorities may decide to limit travel to try to stop the spread of the disease. If this should happen, seven days of food and water may not last long enough for the disease to run its course or for contact with others to be considered safe. You may choose to stock up with enough supplies to last longer than a week for peace of mind or if you think the authorities might not be able to help during the first week after the disaster caused by a terrorist act.

PROTECT FROM TERRORIST DISASTERS

The authorities have declared an Imminent Threat Alert, warning that a terrorist attack is about to happen. This alert tells you what to expect as well as how you might be able to prevent, protect from and respond to the attack. In the event that the attack occurs and creates a disaster, you already know what to do. In previous chapters, you learned about a variety of disaster effects, you prepared ahead of time, and you learned how to protect yourself and others from these effects.

If the terrorist attack occurs and creates a disaster, you act to protect from its effects.

Stay Informed

Follow news about the Imminent Threat Alert and subsequent attack. When the threat alert is issued, watch for alerts from schools and daycare centers so you know if children will need to be picked up early. How much time do you and others have to react once the attack occurs?

Are you in immediate danger? Are the primary disaster effects mobile, stationary, or infectious? Listen to the authorities and check with your long-distance contacts for updates on the dangers you will face and the actions you should take to protect yourself and others.

If you are traveling when you hear about a threat alert, call your long-distance contacts and ask them to help you stay informed. Once the attack occurs, assess whether or not it will affect your travel route, your destination location or your home. Plan to adjust your travel if it does. Act on warnings from the threat alert or for any disaster effects following the attack. Rely on information from both the authorities and your long-distance contacts to decide what to do.

Take Action

The terrorist attack has occurred. You may now be in danger from the attack or any disaster effects it caused. Your first warning may be the sound of sirens, an Internet alert or an emergency broadcast on the radio or TV. If the disaster effects are mobile and threaten your shelter location, like a fire, you must evacuate. Decide whether or not you have time to gather your family or group and evacuate together. Pick up children from schools and daycare centers. If you cannot evacuate together, everyone evacuating separately from the group should call your long-distance contacts. They can coordinate a safe place along the evacuation route where everyone can meet. If you cannot get through by phone, consider texting or posting messages using social media like Facebook or Twitter.

If you are in danger from a toxic gas cloud, evacuation is the best option. If you do not have time to evacuate, you need to stop airflow into your shelter location. Turn off your heating or air conditioning and any fans; close and lock doors; close any vents, including any fireplace dampers. Gather all the people and pets in your family or group into the room you will seal. Consider using a bedroom with a connected bathroom for personal hygiene. Make sure your shelter-in-place kit and emergency radio are with you. Seal all windows, vents and doors to the room using the plastic sheeting and duct tape in your shelter-in-place kit.

You may have to rely on schools or daycare centers to shelter children at their locations. Call any children separated from the group and not in school. If you have no time to evacuate, it may not be safe for them to try to return home. If they cannot return home before the danger arrives, they should shelter where they are or move away from the disaster area, based on whether or not they are in immediate danger.

Periodically check the Internet, radio and TV to get updates on the disaster. Do not unseal your room until the authorities have declared that there is no more danger from the toxic gas cloud.

If the danger is from a disease that is highly contagious, then shelter-in-place. Avoid meeting others who could give you the disease. Follow the guidance from Chapter 11 and protect from this disease just as you would from another highly contagious disease.

Whether you evacuated or sheltered-in-place, check in with your long-distance contacts once you are safe. Let them know your status, which group members are with you, and what injuries you may need medical help treating.

Communicate

When the disaster is over, listen to the news and check the Internet. Are there other threat alerts you need to be aware of? If you were forced to evacuate, can you return home or to where you were staying on vacation? If you sheltered-in-place, check your shelter for damage to make sure it is safe for continued use.

You may have to evacuate if too many essential services will not be restored before you would run out of food and water, or if there is a health hazard, like a radiation leak from a nearby nuclear power plant. If you do not have to evacuate, restock your shelter-in-place and emergency travel kits so you are prepared to respond should another disaster follow shortly after the first one.

Seek medical evaluation and treatment for any injuries that occurred during the disaster.

YOUR CHECKLIST —
TERRORIST DISASTERS

Prepare For Primary Disaster Effects — Terrorist Disasters

❑ Update your emergency kits with additional supplies, including: thick socks and good walking shoes or boots for each person in your group; a portable water-purification device; and solar charger;

❑ Update your emergency shelter-in-place kit with plastic sheeting and duct tape. Consider cutting it to size for the room you will seal;

❑ Plan multiple evacuation routes in case one becomes unsafe;

❑ Make sure your vehicle always has at least half a tank of gas.

Protect From Primary Disaster Effects — Terrorist Disasters

❑ Follow alerts. Pick up children at schools and daycare if you have enough warning time, otherwise, children shelter at their locations;

❑ Evacuate from mobile effects like fire or a toxic gas cloud;

❑ Check the radio and Internet, and talk to your long-distance contacts before and as you evacuate so you can respond to any identified problems with your original evacuation route;

❑ Shelter-in-place from stationary effects or if you cannot evacuate ahead of the disaster effect's arrival:

  ❑ Close and lock doors, close all vents and fireplace dampers;

  ❑ Seal your shelter location if there is a toxic gas hazard;

  ❑ Children who cannot return home safely should shelter where they are or move away from mobile effects;

  ❑ Check the radio and Internet, and talk to your long-distance contacts to make sure it is safe before you unseal your shelter location;

❑ If you shelter-in-place from a highly contagious disease, consider adding enough food and water to your emergency shelter-in-place kit to sustain you, your family or group, and pets for at least two weeks;

❑ Listen for local alerts and hazard warnings. Evacuate if your shelter location cannot protect you from these hazards;

❑ Talk regularly with your local and long-distance contacts. Let them know about any changes in your status, evaluate any new dangers they identify, and decide whether to stay or evacuate based on the new information.

For actions after the disaster, see page 57.

Notes

Notes

Notes

Conclusion

We hope you have found this book to be useful and that it will help you prepare your family or group for the disasters that will come. You do not have to be an expert, but you need to act! Start with family and group discussions and use this book as a resource. You can do this!

Please see Appendix 1, which includes sample emergency kits that can help you better prepare for and protect from different kinds of disasters. Appendix 2 is about response and recovery support from the local level up through the federal government. If you are curious about what kind of support you should expect when recovering from a disaster, this is a good place to start.

Consider getting first-aid training and learning about volunteer opportunities with organizations like the American Red Cross. The training you receive could help your family, friends and neighbors when the unexpected happens.

Good luck,
Jim
Steve
Marc

Appendix 1:
Emergency Kits

Appendix 1 contains sample first-aid, travel and shelter-in-place emergency kit lists for your use. These lists are incomplete because they do not include the special supplies and other items that you and your family or group may need, like certain medications for people or pets, bee-sting kits or glasses.

Please take time to review the lists and add in any current prescriptions and other items you and others need so that your first-aid and emergency kits are complete before you need them.

Store your first-aid kit in a waterproof container. A small kit with a few items could even be stored in a zip-lock waterproof bag.

DISASTER EQUIPMENT AND SUPPLY KITS:

INDIVIDUAL EMERGENCY KIT

Small Daypack with:

1 mask & goggles
1 whistle
1 LED light
2 bottles of water (16 oz)

1 small first-aid kit
1 hand-crank light
1 high-calorie food bar

FAMILY EMERGENCY KIT

Medium Daypack with:
Per person:

1 mask & goggles
1 whistle
1 LED Light
2 bottles of water (16 oz)
1 high-calorie food bar

1 medium first-aid kit
2 hand-crank lights

EVACUATION KIT (RELOCATION)
Medium Daypack with:
Per person:

1 emergency poncho	Toilet paper roll
Hat & pair of gloves	Moist towelette container
2 high-calorie food bars	Hard candy small bag
Toothbrush	Toothpaste
Canteen 2 Qt with water	Hot & Cold Packs
	Insect repellent
	Sunscreen
	Emergency weather radio
	Pet food

SHELTER KIT (SHELTER-IN-PLACE)
Medium Daypack with:

Per person:	2 toilet paper rolls
All-weather blanket	Sleeping bag
8 high-calorie food bars	5 2-gallon water containers
Toothbrush	Waterproof matches box
Canteen 2 Qt with water	Playing cards or travel game
	Toothpaste
Tarp or heavy plastic	Moist towelette container
Duct tape	Hot & Cold Packs
Water-purification tablets box	Pet food

SUSTENANCE KIT (EXTENDED RELOCATION / SHELTER-IN-PLACE)
Large Backpack with:

Per person:	Hand-held water-
4 high-calorie food bars	purification unit
8 bottles of water (16 oz)	Hand-sanitizer wipes
	Solar panel to recharge devices

SUPPLEMENTAL KIT (OPTIONAL EQUIPMENT / SUPPLIES)
Large Backpack with:
Per person:

Eating utensils	Radiac meter	Special refrigerated
Canned and	Shortwave radio	container
dry food	Portable stove	Solar panel to
	Can opener	recharge devices

There is room in the supplemental pack for some individual needs (glasses and medicine for example)

SAMPLE FAMILY OR GROUP FIRST-AID KIT:

FAMILY FIRST-AID

KIT CONTENT	SUGGESTED USE
Absorbent compress 5x9" dressing	Cover/protect open wounds
Adhesive bandages (Assorted Sizes)	Cover/protect open wounds
Adhesive tape (cloth) 1"	Secure bandages or splints
Antibiotic ointment packets (approx 1 g)	Anti-infection
Antiseptic wipe packets	Wound cleaning/germ killer
Aspirin (chewable) 81 mg	Symptoms of a heart attack
Blanket (space blanket)	Maintain body temperature
CPR Breathing Barrier (with one-way valve)	Protection during rescue breathing or CPR
Instant cold compress	To control swelling
Gloves (large), disposable, non-latex	Prevent body fluid contact
Hydrocortisone ointment packets (approx 1 g)	External rash treatment
Scissors	Cut tape, cloth or bandages
Roller bandage 3" (individually wrapped)	Secure wound dressing in place
Roller bandage 4" (individually wrapped)	Secure wound dressing in place
Sterile gauze pad 3x3"	Control external bleeding

FAMILY FIRST-AID

KIT CONTENT	SUGGESTED USE
Sterile gauze pad 4x4"	Control external bleeding
Thermometer, oral (non-mercury/non-glass)	Take temperature orally
Triangular bandage	Sling or binder/splinting
Tweezers	Remove splinters or ticks

(Source: http://www.redcross.org/images/pdfs/code/First_Aid_Kit_Contents.pdf)

Unique Needs:

Add in your prescriptions and other unique needs like a bee-sting kit or contact lens cleaner if you or others do not have an extra pair of glasses. Some first-aid kits also come with a short first-aid booklet. If you have not had any first-aid training or want the ability to refresh your memory, buy a first-aid book if you do not have one, and read it before disaster strikes.

Write in your unique needs below so your first-aid kit and your emergency kits are complete:

_____   _____
_____   _____
_____   _____
_____   _____
_____   _____
_____   _____
_____   _____
_____   _____
_____   _____
_____   _____
_____   _____
_____   _____
_____   _____
_____   _____
_____   _____
_____   _____
_____   _____
_____   _____

Appendix 2:
Recovery Resources

Your prepare and protect actions are your first and best way to avoid or reduce the impact disasters will have on you and others. You are not alone though, and you should expect some help from the local, state, regional and/or federal authorities. Organizations like the American Red Cross may also be able to help. The challenges the authorities and other organizations will have in responding to your needs include: how widespread is the disaster; in what season and where does it occur; and is the U.S. trying to recover from other major disasters that have already happened or may still be happening?

The local, state and federal response to disasters in the U.S. has been carried out many times over the years. Each disaster response is intended to limit the immediate threat to life and safety, prevent suffering and aid in rebuilding. Here is what you can expect, depending upon the size and scope of the disaster.

LOCAL RESPONSE & RESOURCES

First responders are local police, fire and emergency medical personnel. Their capabilities and resources vary, based on where they serve, but all are trained in preparation, response and recovery from disasters. They can have specialized training and equipment, including specific training for disasters common to your area. For example, if you live in the Gulf Coast region, you can expect your first responders to be experienced and skilled in preparation for and recovery from a hurricane. They will assist in evacuations and provide immediate response in the local area when conditions permit.

Many disasters will overwhelm the local response effort and require state and federal resources to respond to the disaster.

State, Regional Response & Resources

Each state and territory of the U.S. has an office of Emergency Management/Security/Civil Defense that provides valuable resources to plan, train and prepare for disasters. When a disaster occurs, they provide management and coordination activities, allowing the state to assist in a disaster response that can go beyond its borders. These offices often establish command and coordination centers to help with the disaster response, which includes requesting resources from nearby states as well as the federal government.

The **Emergency Management Assistance Compact** (EMAC) was established in 1996 to provide mutual aid between states in a time of need. The compact offers assistance when there is a governor-declared state of emergency. It provides a way for states that are not suffering from the effects of a disaster to send resources to states that are suffering, or recovering, from a disaster. These resources include people, equipment and supplies. The compact was ratified by Congress and provides a legal basis for the other states to respond to requests for help, including being paid for the cost of sending resources to states in need of aid. It also addresses legal liabilities and allows for credentials, licenses and certifications to be honored across state lines during the time of a disaster. This compact has improved the speed and overall response to large-scale disasters since 1996, thus saving many lives.

The people, equipment, supplies and services provided through EMAC include:

Fire and Hazardous Material;   Incident Management;
Law Enforcement;   Search and Rescue;
National Guard;   Utility Work;
Emergency Medical Care;   Telecommunications;
Mass Care;   Animal Health Care.
Medical and Public Health;

Federal Response & Resources

The U.S. government has significant resources it can use to respond to large-scale disasters. The federal response is dictated by the National Response Framework (NRF) that provides the legal basis for the response:

"The National Response Framework (NRF) presents the guiding principles that enable all response partners to prepare for and provide a unified national response to disasters and emergencies. It establishes a comprehensive, national, all-hazards approach to domestic incident response."

— *Department of Homeland Security*

The NRF defines the principles, roles and structures that organize how the U.S. responds to large-scale disasters as a nation. The NRF:

- Describes how communities, tribes, states, the federal government, non-governmental partners and private sector work together to provide a broad response;
- Describes specific authorities and best practices for managing incidents;
- Utilizes the National Incident Management System (NIMS) that provides a template for incident response.

To put this is more straightforward terms, this is the format the federal government uses to decide how the authorities will respond to different disasters before they occur. When they occur, the authorities can react more quickly with resources that were identified and, in some cases, moved near the potential disaster area ahead of time. This is the same kind of work you will do to prepare for disasters before they arrive, but on a much larger scale.

How does this work when a disaster occurs? The governor of a state can request federal assistance from the President of the United States through the NRF. The Secretary of the Department of Homeland Security (DHS) is the principal federal officer for domestic incident management, and the Director of the Federal Emergency Management Agency (FEMA) is the primary advisor to the Secretary of DHS and the President. The President gets advice from these leaders and other advisors, and directs the federal government to provide assistance. The primary role of FEMA is to coordinate the response to a disaster that has overwhelmed the resources of state and local authorities. FEMA will respond with resources to help with the response, recovery and rebuilding efforts after a disaster.

The Department of Defense often responds to large-scale disasters to provide Defense Support to Civil Authorities (DSCA). Through the National Response Framework, the president can direct the Secretary of Defense to provide support to civil authorities in a time of need. The United States Northern Command in Colorado Springs, Colorado, directs the defense response to incidents. It is important to note that defense forces work to support civil authorities and are not in charge. They provide critical and often unique defense capabilities that are useful. Without presidential directive under extreme conditions, the defense forces have no authority to police and arrest U.S. citizens. Their focus is to provide help. This help comes with robust capabilities that include, but are not limited to:

Air and ground transportation;
Medical aid and field hospitals;
Air-deployed firefighting capabilities;
Manned and unmanned reconnaissance platforms;
Personnel to assist in search and rescue and delivery aid;

Specialized chemical and radiological units;
Extensive logistical capabilities and support.

The Department of Defense and our nation's military have a long history of providing valuable support when domestic disasters occur.

You will continue to face disasters, regardless of where you live. Authorities at all levels of government in the U.S., as well as volunteers and private organizations like the American Red Cross, will help with disaster recovery. As you plan and prepare for the disasters you and your family or group might face, you can have confidence that, once you survive a disaster through your own efforts, help to rebuild and recover will come.

About the Authors

James D. Lee, P.E. is a West Point graduate and Licensed Professional Chemical Engineer with 30 years of experience in chemical, biological, radiological and nuclear risk management. Since 1998 he has developed vulnerability reduction strategies for Fortune 500 corporations and, as a top consultant for the insurance industry, has implemented his risk-management practices at over 100 locations in 21 countries. He is also the inventor of Purified Hydrogen Peroxide Gas technology.

Steve Healy, B.S., M.S. has more than 10 years of experience in chemical, biological, radiological and nuclear risk management. After leaving the Army, he worked for multiple companies, among them Deloitte, where he spent more than 11 years working in Investment Operations. He is a retired U.S. Army officer and a Northern Illinois University graduate.

Marc Lee, M.S., M.E. has worked extensively with the Department of Defense, Department of Homeland Security and other state and federal agencies in disaster preparedness and response and risk mitigation to critical infrastructure. He is a retired U.S. Army officer and West Point graduate with over 23 years of operational experience.

Acknowledgments

We would like to thank the ladies in our lives — Tiffany, Jennifer, and Karen — as well as our families for their love, support and thoughts as we wrote this book. Thanks also to our publisher for guiding us through the process of bringing this book to you. Finally, a special thanks to Kelly Dickinson for his insight into the CDC, epidemics and pandemics. We hope this book will serve as a great reference to help you better prepare for the unexpected disasters that may come, and to keep you and yours safe!